TE Lawrence and the Red Sea Patrol

Dedicated to June Oliver, whose drawings start each chapter, but who died too soon to see the book.

TE Lawrence and the Red Sea Patrol

The Royal Navy's Role in Creating The Legend

John Johnson-Allen

Pen & Sword
MILITARY

First published in Great Britain in 2015 by
Pen & Sword Military
an imprint of
Pen & Sword Books Ltd
47 Church Street
Barnsley
South Yorkshire
S70 2AS

ISBN 978 1 47383 800 0

Typeset in Ehrhardt by
Mac Style Ltd, Bridlington, East Yorkshire
Printed and bound in the UK by CPI Group (UK) Ltd,
Croydon, CRO 4YY

Pen & Sword Books Ltd incorporates the imprints of Pen & Sword
Archaeology, Atlas, Aviation, Battleground, Discovery, Family
History, History, Maritime, Military, Naval, Politics, Railways,
Select, Transport, True Crime, and Fiction, Frontline Books, Leo
Cooper, Praetorian Press, Seaforth Publishing and Wharncliffe.

For a complete list of Pen & Sword titles please contact
PEN & SWORD BOOKS LIMITED
47 Church Street, Barnsley, South Yorkshire, S70 2AS, England
E-mail: enquiries@pen-and-sword.co.uk
Website: www.pen-and-sword.co.uk

Contents

Acknowledgements   vii

Foreword   ix

Introduction   xiii

Chapter 1   The Red Sea   1

Chapter 2   The Navy   9

Chapter 3   Build Up to the Revolt   33

Chapter 4   The arrival of William Boyle: September 1915–June 1916   49

Chapter 5   The Start of the Revolt: 9 June 1916–30 September 1916   63

Chapter 6   "My Super-Cerebral Friend": October 1916–January 1917   81

Chapter 7   Wejh to Akaba and Beyond: January 1917–December 1918   101

Chapter 8   "When the Time Comes to Tell of It"   121

Appendix 1: The Steam Cutter   127

Appendix 2: HMS Hardinge – *Claim for Freight Payment*   129

Bibliography   133

Index   137

Acknowledgements

For their assistance I would like to thank:

Vice-Admiral Sir Jeremy Blackham KCB for help with the Naval Review and the Foreword.

Captain Jeremy Carew OBE RFA for information and pictures relating to his grandfather.

The Earl of Cork and Orrery for permission to use photographs from the family archive.

Edward Chaplin CMG MVO for sharing his knowledge on the Middle East.

Churchill College Archive Centre, Cambridge, for help with the Wemyss archive.

Commander T. Lilley PhD MA for help with Naval matters of manning.

June Oliver, for her illustrations.

Mr R. Partis for help with steam cutters.

Quotes from Admiralty Pilots and illustrations were sourced from the UK Hygrographic Office.

Ian Killick, Liz Hill and Hannah Newbery of the Hydrographic Department Archive Department were of great and enthusiastic assistance.

Henry Wilson, Matt Jones and Barnaby Blacker of Pen and Sword, for their help and support.

The staff of the National Archive and the British Library.

And lastly, my wife Claire who helped with research and supported me wholeheartedly throughout.

I take all responsibility for errors that may have appeared. All possible effort has been taken, where copyright for illustrations was an issue, to discover the original owner.

Foreword

Jonathan Richard Boyle, Earl of Cork and Orrery

The First World War introduced some unlikely participants to one another and none more so than the relationship which grew up between the Royal Navy and the Arab Nation. The necessity to defend the Suez Canal and to confront the Turkish Ottoman Empire once it had declared its hand as an ally of Germany gave rise to a side-show in Arabia which generated another "sideshow within a side-show" in the form of the Red Sea Patrol. This unique operation, conducted under the auspices of the Commander-in-Chief East Indies station (which perhaps demonstrates the low level of importance attached to it from the beginning), was led through its most important phase by my great uncle, Captain W. H. D. Boyle, who was appointed to command *HMS Fox* in late 1915. In hindsight, it was one of the earliest successful attempts by a maritime power to project its influence inland beyond the littoral along which it was operating. The use of amphibious forces and of air power acting in concert were pioneered in this campaign, and gave rise to the enormous Joint Maritime structures of the second World War, and which we see so often deployed today. Indeed, littoral force projection is one of the main reasons cited today for the construction of new aircraft carriers in the UK.

It is also memorable as the beginning of Arab self-determination, although this was largely overridden by the secret Sykes-Picot agreement of 1916. This agreement arguably led eventually to the conflicts which surround us today. In attempting to ensure that the Arabs rose up and evicted their overlords, the Turks, the British opened the genie's bottle and gave the Middle East an identity. As a means of getting rid of the Turks by proxy this was only partially successful, as British and allied troops did most of the serious fighting, but they were careful to recognise religious sensitivities and to proceed with great caution where matters of custom and culture were concerned. The British had, however, broken the promises earlier made to King Hussein (the Sharif of Mecca) by the governor of Egypt, Sir Henry McMahon. This was later underlined by the Balfour Declaration of 1917.

Boyle was an astute political operator, and had made a point of cultivating excellent contacts within the military and political hierarchies. He was the same age as Churchill and knew him well; many senior Naval Officers fell within his circle of acquaintances, and his wife's family connections were excellent. He was therefore able to use his considerable charm and huge energy to achieve great things. His appointment to *HMS Fox* may have disappointed him ("almost the slowest and oldest ship commanded by a Captain in the Royal Navy") but one can see the thought process at the Admiralty which led to it. He had made a thorough nuisance of himself demanding to be released from his desk job as Naval Attaché in Rome so that he could go to sea and do something which he would have described as useful. The effectively independent Red Sea command was an obvious place to use someone possessing his initiative and energetic character. It also made him especially useful in roles requiring careful political handling. As a result, he was able to conduct one of the most influential maritime campaigns of the War, influencing events ashore with the minimum of force.

The motley collection of ships which characterised the Red Sea Patrol squadron were drawn from a variety of sources, but were surprisingly well suited to their task. The old cruisers had usefully large guns to act as mobile artillery and, more importantly, large crews so that the training and arming of significant landing parties was possible. The armed merchant vessels had a variety of talents, but the three Indian

Marine troopships were ideal for the varied role of transporting stores, troops, animals and passengers. The small monitors which were added in the later stages of the revolt were perfectly suited for guardship duties. The astute use of the relatively new technology of radio (WT) communication made the whole thing possible, since operating along 1,200 miles of coastline would have been very difficult without it. Good relations between senior officers ashore and afloat existed, and the general will to succeed enabled Lawrence to succeed against all the odds in his initial efforts to persuade the various Arab factions to combine into some sort of a whole. The benign and helpful regime established by Admiral Wemyss, the C-in-C East Indies, enabled Boyle to provide the effective support which Lawrence needed. The objectives of the Admiral's command were to secure Egypt, the Red Sea, and the Suez Canal, to project maritime power in the Red Sea Littoral in support of the Arab Revolt, and in particular to wear down the forces of the Turks, and to promote Britain's image as a friend of the Islamic peoples within and without the British Empire. In all of these he succeeded, and was rewarded with the important post of First Sea Lord when he returned to Britain.

It is ironic that today, one hundred years later, the very success of the actions of the Red Sea Patrol in achieving a measure of Arab self-determination, and in improving relationships between Britain and Arabia, is threatened by the sort of religious conflict which Lawrence and Boyle were so careful to avoid. John Johnson-Allen's book is a fascinating tale of intrigue, derring-do and shrewd maritime power projection told from the point of view of the maritime power rather than from the more often viewed perspective of the land operations of TE Lawrence. He has pursued the relatively meagre literary resource with great vigour and it is a worthy read, especially for those students of Levantine politics who seek to understand the origins of the conflicts which confront us today.

21 August 2014

Introduction

On 26 November 1918 the first of three articles appeared, published in *The Times* by "a correspondent who was in close contact with the Arabs" (in accordance with tradition, its contributors then remained anonymous) who was, in reality, TE Lawrence. In the article he gave due credit for the Royal Navy's contribution to the success of the Arab Revolt (although as Malcolm Brown points out, the significance of the naval role was diminished in *Seven Pillars of Wisdom*.[1]) In that article Lawrence noted that "the naval side of the Sherifian operations, *when the time comes to tell of it* [my italics] will provide a most interesting case of the value of command of the sea as a factor in shore operations against an enemy depending entirely on land communications for his maintenance". In writing that, he was not just acknowledging the Navy's part in the success of the Revolt, but also of his own, however reluctantly acknowledged, fame.

In several of the very many books about Lawrence and the Arab Revolt, passing mention is made of the ships of the Red Sea Patrol and their involvement, but until now the naval side of the Red Sea Campaign has not been investigated in detail, and the importance of that aspect of the campaign has gone largely unnoticed, although Jeremy Wilson notes: "In the Hejaz, the Revolt had begun without adequate preparation, and Hussein had only been saved by the Royal Navy."[2] The many other books have been by authors who had no

---

1. TE Lawrence in *War and Peace*, 217.
2. *Lawrence of Arabia*, 412.

particular maritime interest, but had great knowledge in the other areas of the campaign.

I have had a long and abiding interest – as have many, many others – in TE Lawrence and the Arab Revolt. I have had an equally long and abiding interest in maritime history. To be able to combine these two factors to investigate and throw light on a largely unknown operation, which in itself was part of what Lawrence referred to as "a sideshow of a sideshow", was an opportunity I could not let pass.

The Red Sea Patrol was a collection of ships drawn from the Royal Navy, the Royal Indian Marine and some taken up from the Merchant Navy for Royal Naval service. The numbers of ships that took part varied, but more or less numbered twelve. Of that twelve, six were the principal players, with the other six appearing as needed.

The background to the Arab revolt is complicated, but as a starting point, in 1889 in the Ottoman Empire the Committee of Union and Progress (CUP) was formed as a secret protest society consisting mainly of medical and military students. The CUP grew in influence over the next twenty-five years, until on 2 August 1914, two days before Britain declared war on Germany, a decision was forced by a group within the CUP, led by Enver Pasha who was a Germanophile, to form a secret alliance with Germany against Russia. The proximity of the Ottoman Empire to the Suez Canal was naturally a major concern to the British Government and this was underlined in January 1915 when an 80,000 strong Turkish force crossed the Sinai Peninsula to attack the canal, but was beaten off by British forces before it was able to cross the canal. This caused a build-up of British troops in Egypt; by early 1917 a large force under General Allenby moved on a wide front against Turkish forces in Palestine. It was assisted by irregular forces of the Arab Revolt under Feisal, advised, inter-alia, by TE Lawrence.

British opinion on the entry of the Ottoman Empire into the war was concerned by the difficulties over the question of Islamic solidarity. The proclamation of jihad against the Allies was a potential source of unrest in the countries along the route to, and possibly including, India.

Sherif Hussein Ibn Ali, whose family claimed direct descent from the Prophet, was the Emir of Mecca, which was the most prestigious Arab Islamist position within the Ottoman Empire. His main concern was to decide whether his political ambitions would be best served by Turkey or Britain. He had an additional concern caused by the rival interest of Abdul Aziz Ibn Saud, who was based in Riyadh, now the capital of Saudi Arabia. Ibn Saud was promoting Wahhabism, an extremely rigid branch of the Islamist faith, and was offering incentives to tribesmen in the central and eastern part of Arabia to take up the Wahhabi faith. In July 1915 Hussein wrote to the British High Commissioner in Egypt, Sir Henry McMahon, setting out his requirements for him to ally himself to the British. A correspondence between the two followed. The major point of this correspondence was the question of the territories over which Hussein sought power which, in brief, comprised the Arabic speaking lands east of Egypt – the Arabian peninsula, and parts of Iraq and Syria, including Lebanon and Palestine. Eventually Britain agreed to recognise an independent Arab state after the war and to provide supplies, weapons and funds to support the Arab Revolt. Hussein committed himself to an armed revolt against the Turks. The Arab revolt, it was decided, would start on 9 June 1916 at Jeddah, although various Arab military actions started a few days before that.

This book will firstly set the scene, with chapters on the area and the Navy of the time, describing some of the ships and the men, before describing the naval part of the Red Sea Campaign. The last chapter looks at the role and the relevance of the naval side of the Sherifian operation.

The main source for the details of the actions has been the individual ships' deck logs, written at the time by the officer of the watch at the end of his four hour watch. These contemporary records give the most accurate account of events from the naval aspect and correct many statements about the campaign written in other places. These logs were not released until fifty years after the time. They have been supplemented by comments from some of the participants, writing shortly after the end of the war. Not least among these is, of course, TE Lawrence. His description of events brings to life the atmosphere of the time and adds texture to the formal description contained within the ships' logs.

Lawrence wrote:

> "The Red Sea patrol-ships were the fairy-godmothers of the Revolt. They carried our food, our arms, our ammunition, our stores, our animals. They built our piers, armed our defences, served as our coast artillery, lent us seaplanes, provided all our wireless communications, landed landing parties, mended and made everything. I couldn't spend the time writing down a tenth of their services."[3]

Without the Royal Navy's assistance, it will become apparent in this book that in all likelihood, TE Lawrence would have ended the war as just another officer in the army bureaucracy of Cairo.

---

3. TE Lawrence, quoted in "*The Life and Letters of Lord Wester Wemyss*", 359.

Chapter One

The Red Sea

HMS Euralyus

"Now getting worn out, and only good for short spurts." *(Janes, 1914)*

The Red Sea was, until 18 November 1869, a dead end. A long narrow sea bound on either side by desolate wastes, entered through the Straits of Bab-el-Mandeb at its southern end, it runs in a more or less NNW direction, terminating in two narrower fingers: the Gulf of Suez which continues straight and the smaller Gulf of Aqaba which branches off and runs in a direction just east of north. From the head of the Gulf of Suez to the narrow Straits of Bab-el-Mandeb at the southern end it is some 1,200 nautical miles in a nearly straight line.

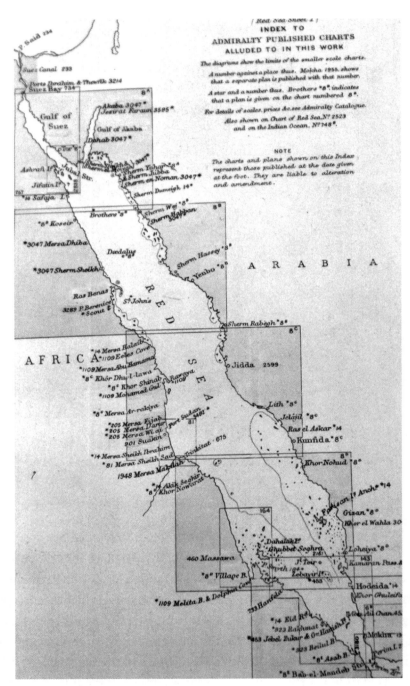

Red Sea. *(Admiralty Pilot 1909)*

From the north the access from the Mediterranean had been by canal, river and then four-horse wagons across an 84-mile stretch of desert. This route, which ran for thirty years from Alexandria to Suez, was operated by P&O Lines to connect with the Suez to Bombay route. The success of the Red Sea end of the operation was the result of the work of Captain John Wilson, who had demonstrated the viability of a route between Suez and Bombay and of Commander Robert Moresby who surveyed the Red Sea between 1829 (only twenty-four years after the Battle of Trafalgar) and 1834. The charts from which his surveys were made were still in use in 1916.

On 18 November 1869, all that changed with the opening of the Suez Canal. The history of the development of the canal can be read elsewhere, but the use of the canal started slowly, only some 430,000 tonnes passing through in the year after it opened. This increased five-fold in the next five years and by 1882 it had risen to over 5,000,000 tons. By 1912 the annual tonnage had reached over 20,000,000 tonnes. In the last five months of 1914 that had reduced by 40 per cent, but even at its lowest point, in 1917, over 8,000,000 tonnes of shipping was still passing annually through the Red Sea. In today's terms this would have equated to some 100 ships, but then it would have been equivalent to about 2,000, ships at the time being very much smaller than today. The Suez Canal of the new millennium is nearly five times wider and three times deeper than in 1869 and accepts ships that were inconceivable in size when it opened, were still inconceivable in 1916, and remained so until after the middle of the next century.

The canal was open to all nationalities, despite the war, for by the 1888 Convention of Constantinople, nine nations, including significantly for what was to follow less than twenty-five years later, Britain, France, Germany, Austria-Hungary, and Turkey, the Suez Canal "shall always be free and open in time of war, as in time of peace to every vessel of commerce or of war, without discrimination of flag".[1] The USA, as

---

1. *Oxford Encyclopaedia of Maritime History*, Vol. 4.

a neutral, benefited and increased its trade through the canal, to the extent that its Hydrographic Office published "the Red Sea and Gulf of Aden Pilot" in 1916.

Having passed through the Suez Canal and through the Red Sea in both directions many times whilst serving in BP Tankers, the author has experienced the weather and moods of the Red Sea for himself. Most of its weather revolves around the words "hot" and "dry". Its weather patterns are influenced by the monsoons of the North Indian Ocean, so from November to March the north–east monsoon weather prevails, and night–time temperatures can be bearable or even pleasant. In June, July and August the South West monsoon is at its peak and the temperatures are furnace-like: maximum daily temperatures in some places can exceed 55°C and normal daily temperatures are about 40°C. Add to that humidity of up to 75 per cent, and the conditions are extremely uncomfortable; in today's air-conditioned ships it is bearable; before that working or sleeping, for Europeans, was much more than *very* uncomfortable. For those who worked in engine rooms and boiler rooms, the temperatures were almost unbearable. The temperatures ashore were even greater. TE Lawrence describes the heat, on arriving in Jeddah in October 1916 on board HMS *Lama*:

> "When at last we anchored in the outer harbour …, the heat of Arabia came out like a drawn sword and smote us speechless."[2]

Another difficulty caused by the climate occurs in the summer, particularly when refraction and mirage effects are common. With the haze caused by dust in the air added to these effects, the combined result can cause navigational problems, rendering sextant sights unsafe, because of the dubious horizon, and significant errors can be and were made in navigation. The dust haze also made visual navigation by shore marks difficult and uncertain. Dust haze and sandstorms are also

---

2. *Seven Pillars of Wisdom* (1922 text) 2003, 47.

experienced in the winter months, when the Khamsin blows. Its effect is reputedly not dissimilar to that of the Southern European mistral on humans: the Arabs have a saying that "when the Khamsin has blown for more than three days, a man is justified in killing his wife". In the summer, katabatic winds blowing down off the mountains can reach up to gale force eight, which can be accompanied by dense dust storms.

The climate affects the salinity of the water: saline evaporation causes a huge loss of water estimated at 900 billion square metres annually, making the Red Sea the most saline of all the world's open seas. This is caused by the narrowness of the opening at the southern end, the Straits of Bab-el-Mandeb, which are only thirteen miles wide. The sea is narrow, being only 190 nautical miles at its widest, with, at the sides, large and shallow coral reefs which restrict the navigational width available to shipping. In the middle of the navigational area lay two prominent coral outcrops which, without appropriate warning, would be serious risks to safe navigation. The first, about ninety miles South South East of the entrance to the Gulf of Suez, is the Brothers, which consists of two coral islets with a lighthouse standing on one of them. The second, a further 100 miles South South East is Daedalus Reef. This is a single small islet, which has deep water on all sides and may be safely passed quite closely. It too has a lighthouse which, in 1916, had an open ironwork framework, painted red, on a masonry base. Both lighthouses were, and still are, manned by crews of lighthouse keepers who were relieved at intervals from their lonely existence in the middle of the Red Sea. These coral outcrops are on the top of sub-sea peaks, rearing up from the bottom of the central trough which is over 2000m deep; this depth is continued into the Gulf of Aqaba. The two gulfs at the northern end are divided by the Sinai peninsular which is a mountainous desert area, rising in the south to over 2500m. The Gulf of Suez, although larger and wider, is much shallower. The depth of the Gulf of Aqaba, which is similar to the depth in the main part of the sea, is evidence that it and the Red Sea are part of the Great Rift Valley, which runs from the Jordan Valley at its northern end to its southern end, south of the Equator; the Red Sea forms the greatest part of that length.

In addition, evidence of relatively recent volcanic activity in the more southern part has been found with many islands in this part being the top of volcanic cones. A very detailed account of the topography is given by Cyril Crossland, who was the Marine Biologist to the Government of Sudan, in his book written in 1913. In addition to the geography of the Red Sea, he writes in detail of the western side of the Red Sea, its people and its coral reefs. On his first visit to Port Sudan he describes his impression of the mountains and the littoral plain in 1913 as a "great and terrible wilderness" and "a naked savage land".[3] Added to that, the offshore coral reefs made approaching the coast very difficult. The Eastern, Arabian shore, is not greatly different; Crossland's description of a "naked savage land" of the Western shore is also a fair reflection of the nature of the Eastern Shore. It has extensive coral reefs off shore, and the harbours then were no more than inlets between reefs and only approachable at certain times of day. There had been some improvement by 1915 as some buoys and beacons had been established, but navigation near the coast remained both difficult and dangerous. Operating near the coast, the ships of the Red Sea Patrol had virtually all been aground at some stage. Since then, there have been several Port developments on the eastern side during the latter part of the last century with, for example, Rabegh having a large oil terminal; Jeddah now has a container terminal and a livestock terminal within the port area and offshore oil production platforms. On the western shore at the northern end, on the Egyptian coast, holiday resorts have been developed, for example at Sharm-el-Sheikh.

The majority of the sailors in this hot, often windy, savage area in the early part of the twentieth century were Arabs. The native population of the West Coast restricted their nautical activities to fishing from canoes. Local trade up and down the Red Sea and from side to side was predominantly undertaken by dhows, or sambuks as they were alternatively known on the West Coast, which were principally based in the area of Jeddah. These craft were less than efficient sailing

---

3 *Desert and Water Gardens of the Red Sea*, 2.

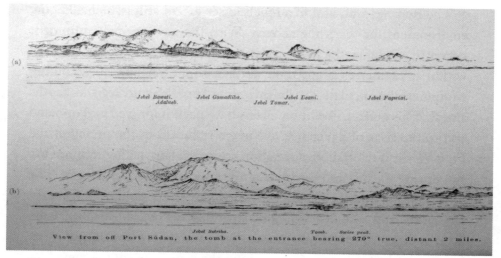

View of Port Sudan. *(Admiralty Pilot 1909)*

vessels, having a shallow draft, being principally open and with a lateen main sail of cotton canvas; beating to windward in particular was not efficient. Some carried a mizzen mast but the mizzen sail was rarely set. Despite their limitations they were, however, good sea boats and Crossland commented that "despite the extreme clumsiness of the rig and the apparently haphazard way the numerous half naked sailors tumble over one another and yell like Babel when anything has to be done they are cleverly handled."[4] The Arabs were also involved in pearl fishing throughout the Red Sea, in dhows and also in smaller craft. The dhow, or sambuk, carried dugout canoes from which the actual pearl fishing was carried out, a system which has echoes of the methods of the fishing fleets on the Grand Banks off Newfoundland. The dhow was little changed in design from the eighteenth century; illustrations of similar ships have been noted on a chart dated about 1790.[5]

4. *Desert and Water Gardens of the Red Sea.*
5. "Depiction of Indo-Arabic Charts on an Eighteenth Century Chart", *Mariners Mirror.*

The Red Sea was, and to a much lesser extent still is, a challenging environment for maritime activity. With the navigational equipment currently available, the present day navigator can know his position to within a few metres at any time, and has sophisticated echo sounding equipment to calculate depth, including being able to see the depths ahead of his craft. In addition charts have been improved and updated and so the risks of navigation are much reduced. In the period of the First World War, offshore navigation was by sextant, taking sights of the sun during the day and the stars at morning and evening twilight. The uncertain horizons reduced the accuracy of those sights significantly. Closer to land visual navigation depended on charts that had been little updated since the previous century, and taking bearings of shore features in dust laden air. Carrying out the same procedures some fifty years later the author can vouch for the degree of uncertainty that existed. Assessing the depth before the advent of the echo sounder still relied on the hand and lead line; not inaccurate, but slow, although having the benefit of being able to discover the nature of the bottom from the tallow armed lead, which the echo sounder could not tell. Groundings then were not uncommon close to the coast; it says much for the skill of the navigating officers on the ships of the Royal Navy that there were not more groundings than recorded.

An example of the navigation close to the coast comes from the log of HMS *Fox*, for 5 January 1916. She was on passage from Jidda to Ras Malek, a small inlet approximately seventy miles[6] to the North. At 0715[7] breakers were noted on the starboard bow, so she altered course 33 degrees to port. An hour and a half later, a reef was sighted ahead, so she altered 40 degrees to starboard, which took her almost back to her original course. A caution noted on the chart for the area states that "the positions of the reefs ... are approximate only".

---

6. All distances at sea will be given in nautical miles.
7. Ship's times will be shown on 24 hour notation.

Chapter Two

The Navy

HMS Fox

"Almost the slowest & oldest ship commanded by a Captain in the Navy." *(Boyle)*

I n the ninety-five years from the Battle of Trafalgar to the turn of the twentieth century the Royal Navy had seen the change from sail to steam, which had been resisted by some Naval officers. Change had come, although it was untested by action. In the decades of peacekeeping, the "Pax Britannica" of the nineteenth century, the power of the British Empire was enforced by its unchallenged maritime supremacy. Minor actions had taken place in various distant parts of the world, but there was no major naval action of any sort until the battle of Tsuchima, in the Russo-Japanese war, in 1895, at which Royal Naval officers were present as observers on the ships of the Japanese Navy. The change to steam brought a new breed of men to the Royal Navy – the engineer. Engineers were regarded by Naval Officers as inferior. Before steam, officers had understood the ships completely. Now, "the real masters of the Navy were the despised engineers, whose mammas were not asked to tea by other mammas."[1]

Admiral Sir John "Jacky" Fisher, whose words they were, was the great Naval reformer in the first decade of the twentieth century. He brought much more to the post then many other naval officers would have done. A friend not only of King Edward VII but also of Lord Selborne, First Lord of the Admiralty, he wielded power (in some historians' view, in a dictatorial manner). His appointment in 1904 as First Sea Lord was the start of a period of profound and controversial change in the Royal Navy. He brought about major changes in the training of officers and initiated a major shift in ships and equipment. The Royal Navy was spread all over the world with its ships grouped into three commands. The main fleets were the Home Fleet and Channel Squadron, Mediterranean Fleet and the Far Eastern Fleet. In order to fulfil the needs of the Empire a great number of ships of varying types, from gunboats to cruisers and battleships, were required. However, many ships were, in the words of Lord Selborne, who introduced Fisher's reforms to the Cabinet on 6 December 1904, "too old to fight and too slow to run away".[2] He concluded by saying that "a certain number of ships of comparatively small value have been or will be withdrawn from commission". He did not say that his intention was to remove 154 ships from the Navy List. The purpose of this was to release officers and men for redeployment to the new ships

---

1. Quoted in *The Fleet That Jack Built*, 106.
2. Selborne "*Memorandum*", quoted in Nicolas A Lambert "*Sir John Fisher's Naval Revolution*", 99.

being built. It released 950 officers and 11,000 men.[3] In addition to the men who were deployed into the ships that were being built, many men were moved into manning older ships that had been put into the reserve fleet. Some of these obsolete ships were, however, scrapped to save money; at the time the saving was £845,000 per annum.[4]

This was a part of his overall policy. He believed, as it turned out correctly, that Germany was a much more likely enemy than France or Russia, which were the perceived enemies of many politicians of the period. Fisher's intentions "were to concentrate the cream of the fleet where it belonged",[5] that is to say in home waters, even at the risk of weakening British influence in other more distant waters. Fisher intended to use the fleet as a weapon of deterrence to act against German strategic concerns, putting pressure on through the anti-German section of the British press. An anti-German article also appeared in the French newspaper *Le Matin*. His actions did not go unnoticed; in Germany he was accused of "bizarre bellicosity".

The Ships

The Red Sea Patrol was formed by a mixture of Royal Navy and Royal Indian Marine ships. The Royal Indian Marine, the precursor of the Royal Indian Navy, gained that title in 1892. Previously it was called Her Majesty's Indian Marine but had been renamed in recognition of its loyal service in the previous decade. Despite its title it was not Royal, as its officers did not hold a Royal commission, nor was it properly Indian because there were no Indian officers until the 1920s. The executive officers in the war period were all British, the engineers and warrant officers were Mauritian or Eurasian and the sailors Indian.[6] In 1892 its officers were British and the senior officers numbered two captains and

3. Adml J Fisher, quoted in "*Sir John Fishers Naval Revolution*" 112.
4. "*Sir John Fishers Naval Revolution*" 125.
5. Arthur Marder quoted in "*Sir John Fishers Naval Revolution*", 101.
6. Rear Adml K Sridharan, *A Maritime History of India*, 237.

seventeen commanders, eleven of whom were in shore appointments. During the war the numbers of the Royal Indian Marine increased to 500 officers and 13,000 sailors. It was not a combatant service until the war; the ships, although lightly armed, were engaged in logistical work as troopships in support of Royal Naval operations. Its three troopships, *Dufferin, Northbrook* and *Hardinge* were all built in Great Britain between 1900 and 1907 and were occupied in troop carrying until 1914. At the outbreak of war they were converted to auxiliary cruisers, re-armed and re-commissioned as Royal Naval ships, with Royal Naval and Royal Indian Marine officers and mainly Indian crews. In addition to the three troopships, other Royal Indian Marine ships were requisitioned, including the *Minto*, built in 1893, which became an occasional part of the Red Sea Patrol. Some merchant ships were requisitioned as Armed Boarding Steamers. Two of these were from the British India Steam Navigation Company, the *Lunka* and *Lama*, which joined *Dufferin, Hardinge, Northbrook* and *Minto*. Apart from the *Minto*, the RIM ships were more up to date than the ships that the Royal Navy provided.

The Admiral's flagship, HMS *Euryalus*, was built in 1901, the last of a class of obsolete four funnelled cruisers which included *Cressy, Aboukir* and *Hogue*. Those three ships were sunk in the southern North Sea by the German submarine, U9, with the loss of nearly 1,500 men and boys on 22 September 1914, not long after the outbreak of war. Of the cruisers that were in the Patrol, *Minerva* was built in 1895 and *Fox* in 1893. The word cruiser, as applied to *Fox* and *Minerva* gives an impression of more power than, at the time, was the case. A cruiser was a much smaller ship than the larger and more powerful ship which had evolved by World War Two and was more akin in size to a World War Two Fleet destroyer. It had evolved in the latter part of the nineteenth century to do precisely what its name suggested; to cruise and protect shipping and the Pax Britannica. Although the nominal top speed of the cruisers was 19 to 20 knots, Jane's Fighting Ships of 1914 notes, for example, that the *Euryalus* class was "now getting worn out and only good for short spurts".[7] Similar comments are noted for the other cruisers. Captain William Boyle (of whom more later) on his appointment to command the *Fox*, commented "The *Fox* was almost the slowest and oldest ship commanded by a Captain in the Royal Navy."[8]

Looking in more detail, firstly, at the *Fox* and the *Minerva*, the former was one of a class of eight; by 1914 one had become an unarmed depot ship and two more had been struck off the list, presumably scrapped. Of just under 4,500 tons she was armed with two 6-inch guns forward and aft and eight 4.7-inch guns mounted in casemates on the sides. This layout was typical of the older cruisers and battleships, before the advent of revolving turrets; the guns on the sides had a limited area of operation. (The illustration on p.1 of the plate section of the restored Russian cruiser *Aurora*, moored in St Petersburg, shows side mounted casemate guns.) She also carried three torpedo tubes. When first built her top speed was 19.5 knots, which was supplied by coal burning engines; she could carry 1,000 tons of coal. However by 1915 her top speed had significantly reduced, as Captain Boyle's comment makes clear. With two funnels and a ram bow, she was typical of the design of the period. The *Minerva*, slightly more recent than the *Fox*, was also somewhat larger at just over 5,500 tons and more heavily armed, with eleven 6-inch guns, one forward of the bridge, two more on the after deck and eight in side casemates. She also had sixteen smaller guns. Her design top speed (when built) and coal storage was the same as *Fox;* a note in Jane's Fighting Ships 1914 indicated that, by then, the top speed could only be sustained for short periods.[9] Visually, with her ram bow, two funnels and tall masts she was very similar.

The three sloops, *Clio, Espiegle* and *Odin* had been built between 1900 and 1903 and still had masts and yards for sails, although no sails

---

7. *Janes Fighting Ships 1914*, 61.
8. *My Naval Life*, 94.
9. *Janes Fighting Ships 1914*, 74.

were carried by the time of the outbreak of war. The *Espiegle* of the Royal Navy and the *Minto* of the Royal Indian Marine were similar in appearance. Classed as sloops they had more the appearance of private steam yachts. They had clipper bows, tall masts and white hulls. *Espiegle* was armed with six 4–inch guns, so for her size was well armed.

The three Royal Indian Marine troopships, which became auxiliary cruisers in the Royal Navy, were significantly larger; the *Dufferin*, at 7,500 tons was the largest of the three. *Northbrook* was only eight years old. *Hardinge* was the oldest. They were all twin funnel ships with raked bows and were armed with 4–inch or 4.7–inch guns. The particular value of these three ships, given their size and purpose, is illustrated by TE Lawrence in a description of *Hardinge*:

> "She was an Indian troopship and her lowest troop–deck had great square ports all along ... We stuffed straight into them 8000 rifles, 3 million rounds of ammunition, thousands of shells, quantities of rice and flour, a shed full of uniforms, two tons of high explosive and petrol ... It was like posting letters in a box."[10]
>
> (But with high explosive and petrol in the same space, somewhat more risky.)

Lunka and *Lama* were two of the Armed Boarding Steamers. Both were taken into service by the Royal Indian Marine from the British India Steam Navigation Company but became part of the Royal Navy for the war period. Two of a class of four, they were relatively small (at just over 2,000 tons) cargo/passenger ships carrying about forty–one first and second–class passengers in cabins, and many more passengers on the open decks. They were built specifically for the Indian trade, with steam turbine engines, capable of over 19 knots. *Lunka* had been employed on the Calcutta/Rangoon route for ten years; the *Lama* had

---

10. *Seven Pillars of Wisdom*, 135.

been on the Bombay/Karachi run for the same period.[11] This trade, carrying cargo and passengers, including many deck passengers, around the Indian coast continued as an integral part of British India's operations in the East up until the 1960s. Although these two ships had been taken up into the Royal Navy, they clearly had retained the fittings from their pre-war trade, including the armchairs on the upper deck. Lawrence and Ronald Storrs joined the *Lama* in Suez to take passage to Jeddah:

> "The atmosphere was like a bath. The scarlet leathers of the armchairs on the *Lama*'s deck had dyed Storrs' white tunic and trousers as bright as themselves in the damp contact of the last four days ... I was wondering if everything he sat on would grow scarlet like himself."[12]

The *Suva* was also taken up as an Armed Boarding Steamer; she had been built in 1906 for the Australasian United Steam Navigation Company to carry passengers and, principally, bananas between Fiji and Sydney. However in 1915 she was converted and fitted with three 4.7-inch guns. Slower than the British India ships, she could make a top speed of 14 knots. After conversion, with the intention of her employment in the Red Sea, on her arrival at Aden she was sent back to Colombo as unsuitable. Whilst there, her Australian crew was replaced by a Royal Naval one and she returned to the Red Sea, where she remained for the next three years.[13]

Two other ships require mention. Although not part of the Red Sea Patrol they provided a further element of support to the Arab Revolt which was, for the place and period, revolutionary. The *Ben-my-Chree*

---

11. *Merchant Fleets: British India Steam Navigation Company*, 91.
12. *Seven Pillars of Wisdom*, 48.
13. "HMS Suva, Captain WHD Boyle and the Red Sea Patrol 1916–18: the strategic effects of an Auxiliary Cruiser upon the Arab Revolt" in *The International Journal of Naval History*.

and the *Anne* were seaplane carriers, and provided occasional support in the Red Sea for specific operations. The use of seaplanes carried by ships had only started in October 1914 when a scheme to attack the Zeppelin sheds at Cuxhaven had been attempted as part of the operations of Sir Reginald Tyrwhitt's Harwich Force. It had failed: because of a heavy rainstorm, the planes, once launched into the sea, had been unable to take off. Undaunted, another attempt was put in place, but the North Sea in October is not the place to seek a smooth sea and it and subsequent similar operations before Christmas that year all failed.[14] In May 1915, a fresh raid was planned on Norddeich, and the *Ben-my-Chree* was one of the ships involved, carrying seaplanes in that operation. Once again the wind was too great. Three days later it was dense fog that prevented the attack, in addition to causing a collision between the destroyer HMS *Lennox* and *Ben-my-Chree*.[15] Two weeks later she was sent to the Dardanelles and, after the end of that disastrous operation she moved to Port Said. Whilst there she was in another collision, this time with the British India ship *Uganda*, which caused significant damage to the *Ben-my-Chree*'s bow. After repairs, she commenced her occasional services in the Red Sea, operating from Aden as well as Port Said, at the northern end of the Suez Canal. After a prolonged series of misfortunes, the conditions in the Red Sea were, as will be seen, more suited to seaplane operations. She had been built as an Irish Sea ferry for the Isle of Man Steamship Packet Company in 1907. Fitted with steam turbine engines and three propellers her top speed was over 24 knots. In 1915 she was one of two ships of that company that were converted to seaplane carriers, the other being the *Viking*, which was renamed HMS *Vindex*. In *Ben-my-Chree*'s case she retained her original name. Part of her after superstructure was removed, in order to make a hangar big enough to house six seaplanes. A crane was fitted to lift the planes in and out

---

14. "Tyrwhitt of the Harwich Force", 83.
15. Ibid, 121.

of the water. Additionally a 60-foot platform for launching from the foredeck was constructed, although the means of moving the planes from the after hangar to the foredeck is not clear. She was also armed with 12-pounder guns. In operation, she became very efficient, able to embark or disembark a seaplane in under a minute. The *Anne* was one of two German merchant ships which were captured in Port Said. Under the German flag her name had been the *Aenne Rickmers*. (The other was the *Rabenfels*, which was also renamed and became the *Raven II*). She had initially been requisitioned and operated under the Red Ensign with her original name, before being torpedoed in 1915 by a Turkish torpedo-boat. After repairs she was transferred to the Royal Navy and renamed HMS *Anne*. She only carried two seaplanes, despite being of 7,000 tons, and had a top speed of only 10 knots. Larger, very much slower, and minimally equipped, she was clearly a very inferior sister to the *Ben-my-Chree*.

The monitors *M31* and *Humber* had an important part to play at the latter end of the campaign. Monitors were small ships (*M31* was under 600 tons) with a shallow draft which could lie inshore to act as heavy artillery in support of land operations, and carried very large guns for their size, normally 6-inch, which were the main armament of a cruiser. They were used as guard ships, stationed in a port. Slow and cumbersome, they were unsuited to patrolling. They were not "amphibious assault vessels", as Michael Asher describes them.[16]

All the ships of the Red Sea Patrol were coal burning. The replenishment of the coal bunkers was a filthy and unpleasant job. David Gregory, in *The Lion and the Eagle*, gives an excellent description of the task:

"Coaling ship was the bane of shipboard life in the ironclad era … For the best part of a day, sometimes longer, the entire crew

---

16. *Lawrence, the Uncrowned King of Arabia*, 194. He also described *Dufferin* as a battleship.

of the [receiving ship] would manhandle thousands of sacks of coal on board and down to the nether regions of the vessel. There, the sacks would be broached and the contents shovelled into coal bunkers. It was backbreaking work and, at the end of the process, the crew would be utterly exhausted. Coal dust would be everywhere in the air, and the entire ship coated in a layer of black filth. A further full days work by the crew would be required to clean up the mess … The sheer awfulness of the experience in the tropics can well be imagined. In the latter case, coaling would often take several days due to crew exhaustion, during which time the ship would of course be non-operational."

The men

The crews of these ships were a very mixed bunch. Some were regular Royal Navy, some Fleet Reserve, some Royal Naval Reserve and some Royal Indian Marine. Some were British and some Indian. All the ships flew the White Ensign of the Royal Navy as, if not already Royal Naval ships, they had become so under the requisitioning that took place. Before the war, the ships of the Royal Indian Marine flew the Blue Ensign; the Merchant Navy ships the Red Ensign. Both Royal Indian Marine and British India Steam Navigation ships had British officers and Indian crews. On the *Lama* and the *Lunka*, the two merchant ships requisitioned from the British India Steam Navigation Company Ltd, all the officers were of the Royal Naval Reserve, with the exception of the captain, who was a Royal Naval officer. Whether the officers had been British India officers previously is unknown, but the policy of the company was not to encourage officers to join the Royal Naval Reserve. The nature of British India's trading was that the majority of their ships were away from the United Kingdom for over two years at a time. This presented difficulties for Reserve officers who would need to be able to return to the United Kingdom to keep up their training commitments.

The Navy List is a comprehensive list of all naval officers, and ships of the Royal Navy, with, inter alia, other Commonwealth navies and, in time of war, Merchant Ships requisitioned for naval purposes. The Navy List of December 1916 (it is an annual publication) gives details, amongst the many thousands of ships listed, of all those on the Red Sea Patrol. For the *Lama* it shows that Acting Commander Charles Scott was in command – he who had taken Lawrence from Suez to Jidda (see Chapter 1) and had a Lt Commander John Robertson RNR as his next in command. Robertson had most probably been the ship's master in peacetime, retained for his knowledge of the ship and given a temporary RNR commission to enable him to stay on board. The other officers, three lieutenants and a midshipman, three engineer officers and radio telegraphist were all shown as RNR. All the other personnel on board would have been Eurasian or Indian. The *Lunka* was commanded by Acting Commander Malcolm Murray, with Lt Commander Reginald White RNR as his second-in-command; again, all the other officers and engineers were RNR officers. The *Suva* had as her regular captain Commander Henry Peel Ritchie, although in December 1916 Captain William Boyle was in command. As Senior Naval Officer, he had moved to the *Suva* for the period that the *Fox* had gone to Bombay for dry dock. Ritchie was the first Naval Officer to win a Victoria Cross in World War One for his gallantry on a raid in Dar es Salaam in East Africa, in 1914. In the course of the raid he was severely wounded, but recovered sufficiently to take command of the *Suva*. He retired in 1917 because of his health. He lived until 1958 taking no further part in any matters naval. By a coincidence, one of the ships that was supporting the action in Dar es Salaam was HMS *Fox*.

Both the *Ben-my-Chree* and *Anne*, as former merchant ships, were requisitioned and came into the same category of the Navy List as the *Lama*, *Lunka* and *Suva*. However the manning of the *Ben-my-Chree* was very different. In her role as a seaplane carrier she had a large number of officers, with, in command, Charles Samson who was a Wing

Commander in the Royal Naval Air Service. He had two immediate subordinates of equal rank: Squadron Commander Cecil J. L'Estrange-Malone RNAS and Lieutenant Commander Arthur Barber RNR. The latter, an experienced Reserve officer would have had responsibility for the ship; L'Estrange-Malone for the aircraft and aircrew. Samson had volunteered for the RNAS in 1904 and L'Estrange-Malone in 1911. Samson had not been at sea since 1904 and had no recent or executive seagoing experience since that time, when he was a young lieutenant. There were twenty-four other officers, split between deck officers, aircrew and engineers. All the deck and engineer officers were Royal Naval Reserve, with the exception of one seconded army officer who was an aircraft observer. In the post-war period, having left the service, this officer entered Parliament and by 1929 had become the Secretary of State for India. He was Lieutenant Wedgwood Benn, the father of Anthony Wedgwood Benn. The crew of the *Ben-my-Chree* would, for the most part, have been her original deck and engine room hands engaged on T124 terms (see below). The Merchant Navy men so engaged were of a very different type to the trained Naval rating. Captain R.S. Gwatkin-Williams CMG RN was put in command of an Irish Sea ferry, the *Hibernia* which, before the war, had run between Holyhead and Dublin. On her transfer to the White Ensign she was renamed HMS *Tara*. He described her crew thus:

"By any means, the crew of the *Tara* could [not] be called fighting men. Both officers and men were the railway company's old employees … The older members of the crew were decent staid individuals, long in the service of the company … The 50% of novices added to them were, for the most part, scallywags and corner boys dragged up anyhow from anywhere … All alike were equally ignorant of firearms, and, if the truth must be confessed, were as frightened of guns as a monkey of snakes. However, they had for the most part been born and bred to the sea, and consequently were not over-prone to sea-sickness, and could be sent aloft to the crows-nest and look-out duty without falling down and hurting themselves."[17]

By way of contrast, the *Anne,* which carried only two seaplanes, had Lt John Kent RNR in command, with three deck officers and one engineer officer, all of whom were Royal Naval Reserve. Lastly, of the requisitioned merchant ships, the *Suva* had all Reserve officers and a Royal Naval crew. This crew had replaced her Australian crew before her service in the Red Sea started. It is open to speculation whether her original Australian Merchant Navy crew had signed on to sail on the ship on T124 articles of agreement.

The T124 agreement was a six-month fixed agreement which was specific to a particular ship, introduced for wartime requirements. At the end of the six months many crews who had signed on these conditions were dissatisfied, because it had not been made apparent that by so doing they had placed themselves under the Naval Discipline Act. Further, those who had not signed on under such an agreement and stayed in merchant ships were to receive war bonus payments not payable to those under T124 terms. When the initial six-month agreement came to an end the new agreement was to serve on any ship without limit of time. This was, naturally, unpopular so it could be conjectured that this was what precipitated the change of crew on the *Suva.*

Of the Royal Navy ships, *Espiegle,* the sloop, as befitted her small size had a small crew by naval standards. Below Commander Ernest Betts RN, her captain, were three RNR officers, a surgeon and three warrant officers. The remainder of the crew were all regular Royal Navy ratings. The *Fox* was the Senior Naval Officer's ship, normally under the command of Captain William Boyle, although at the end of 1916 she was commanded by Commander H.P. Ritchie. Of her nine officers at that time, only two were RNR. At that time *Fox* was on her

---

17. *Under the Black Ensign,* 11.

way to Bombay for dry dock and a refit. Similarly, *Minerva* had the same number of officers as the *Fox* of whom only four were RNR. Her captain, Cecil Raikes had joined the ship a week after she was commissioned on June 12 1914. She had been in the reserve fleet so had to be put into seagoing order, stored with coal and ammunition and a full crew put on board. She sailed on 18 July 1914 to join the Spithead Review of the Fleet as part of a trial mobilisation. A week later the signal for the demobilisation was given, following the review, and the dispersal of the Third Fleet of which the elderly *Minerva* was a part. Twenty-four hours later came the news of Serbia's rejection of Austria's ultimatum following the assassination of Archduke Ferdinand in Sarajevo. The demobilisation was halted immediately, but it was too late for *Minerva*'s crew, who had been trained up over the previous month and had now left the ship. A completely new crew joined and the training started once again.[18]

The *Dufferin*, *Northbrook* and *Hardinge*, the three troopships of the Royal Indian Marine, now commissioned in the Royal Navy as auxiliary cruisers, all were commanded by Royal Navy Commanders with officers split between regular Royal Navy and Royal Naval Reserve and an equal number of Royal Indian Marine officers. The little *Minto*, of the same size as the *Espiegle*, had a Royal Navy officer in command and a Royal Naval Reserve second in command; all her other officers were from the Royal Indian Marine.

Three of the Royal Navy officers went on from their service in the Red Sea, although, as Boyle commented, cut off from the main scenes of naval activity[19], to achieve the highest rank in the Navy, that of Admiral of the Fleet.

Joining the *Minerva* in 1914, Lt Bruce Fraser had become her gunnery officer. He had joined the Navy as a cadet in 1902, at the age of 14. After training at HMS *Britannia*, the Royal Navy's cadet

---

18. *Fraser of North Cape*, 33.
19. *My Naval Life*, 94.

ship, in the days before the Royal Naval College was built, he joined his first ship, HMS *Hannibal*, a month before his 16th birthday. In 1912 he was appointed to the shore base, HMS *Excellent*. By that time he had been promoted to lieutenant and was joining the Navy's Gunnery School. *Excellent* was "the fount of authority of the Navy's drill and ceremonial, demanding the highest standards in immaculate precision".[20] He left there in 1914 having completed the course and become an instructor. He went from the rigid ceremonial and formal ways of the Gunnery School to a very elderly cruiser which had just come from the reserve fleet. He stayed with the *Minerva* until early 1916, when he returned to the Gunnery School briefly, before being posted as Gunnery Officer to the latest dreadnought to join the Grand Fleet, HMS *Resolution*. His career continued on a steady upward course, through the post war reductions of the Navy until, in 1938, he was appointed Rear Admiral, becoming Third Sea Lord one year later. His upward progression continued: in 1942 he was appointed second in command of the Home Fleet, becoming Commander in Chief the next year. In 1943 he was in command of the fleet at the Battle of the North Cape and the sinking of the *Scharnhorst*. Flying his flag from the battleship *Duke of York*, the battle culminated in the destruction of the *Scharnhorst* on Boxing Day 1943. Following that he went to the Far East for the remainder of the war with the Eastern Fleet. In 1948 he succeeded to the highest position in the Navy, as First Sea Lord, being appointed Admiral of the Fleet in October 1948. He was held in huge regard by all his officers and men throughout his service. This was expressed by Colin White:

> "the spirit of the real Nelson ... was much in evidence in the Second World War. It was seen in the remarkable dash and courage in the face of impossible odds, in battles such as the armed merchant man *Jervis Bay*'s lonely and gallant fight with the heavy cruiser

---

20. *Fraser of North Cape*, 25.

Hipper [sic] ...[21] It was present in the love which officers and men alike felt for Bruce Fraser."[22]

Captain William "Ginger" Boyle, who was Senior Naval Officer of the Red Sea Patrol and in command of HMS *Fox*, was the second officer who rose to become Admiral of the Fleet. Described as short of stature and short of temper – the latter matching his red hair – he was a highly regarded officer. He had joined HMS *Britannia*, the Royal Navy's cadet training ship, moored at Dartmouth, in December 1886. After his two years there, he was appointed midshipman to HMS *Monarch*, at that time one of the most modern ships in the Navy, with her four main guns mounted in turrets, although they were still muzzle-loaded. She still had fully rigged masts as the Navy felt it was not yet safe to send ships on long passages without sails. The shipboard food of those last days of the nineteenth century still included salt beef and salt pork with weevil infested biscuits. A welcome addition to the diet was corned beef. Boyle noted:

"Later in life I was in the fleet and a general signal was made ordering a certain 'lot' of corned beef to be destroyed as a human finger had been found in it. One of the admirals present signalled to request that he might be informed whether it was a thumb of the right hand. He had lost that finger some years before."[23]

His career progressed up through the ranks in the quiet and peaceful days at the end of the nineteenth century and the start of the twentieth century. Just before the end of the nineteenth century he was appointed

---

21. Not the *Hipper*, a heavy cruiser, but the *Admiral Scheer*, a pocket battleship. The result was the same.
22. "The Nelson Companion": *The Immortal Memory*, 28.
23. *My Naval Life*, 19.

to HMS *Daphne*, a sloop with twin propellers but barquentine[24] rigged. When he became Senior Naval Officer of the Red Sea Patrol he found HMS *Espiegle* & *Minto* as part of his command, and almost identical to the *Daphne* in appearance.

He was promoted Captain in 1913 and took up a posting as Naval Attaché in Rome. This posting also covered the countries of Austria, Turkey and Greece. Before he left, as part of his induction as a Naval Attaché, he visited the Naval flying school at Sheerness where Commander Samson, who was to command *Ben-my-Chree* in the Red Sea, was in charge. He was still in his post in Rome at the outbreak of World War I in 1914, but by 1915 was desperate to leave. He visited the Mediterranean Fleet which served to increase his frustration:

"It was my first glimpse of the British Navy under war conditions. I had been serving for nearly 30 years trying to be prepared for that day and to find myself in a backwater when it arrived was almost more than I could bear."[25]

He had to wait until September of that year before he was appointed to the *Fox*. His time in Rome had been a success: for "valuable service" he was awarded the Italian decoration of Commander of the Order of St Morris and St Lazarus, in March 1916. His time in the Red Sea will be dealt with, in detail, in subsequent chapters.

In October 1917 he was posted to command HMS *Repulse*, the flagship of the First Battlecruiser Squadron, part of the Grand Fleet, operating in the North Sea. After two years in the climate of the Red Sea, the temperatures were going to be very different. So was the ship: under a year old, the *Repulse* was a 32,000 ton ship with six 15-inch guns, a top speed of over thirty knots, over 900 foot long, and with a

---

24. A barquentine is square rigged on the foremast, and fore and aft rigged on the main and mizzen masts.
25. *My Naval Life*, 89.

crew of over 1,000 (the *Fox* had 320). Promoted to Rear Admiral in 1924 he was then appointed to the Atlantic Fleet, flying his flag on board the battleship HMS *Resolution*. Five years later he was appointed to be President of the Royal Naval College Greenwich, described in those days as the Navy's University. He was succeeded at Greenwich by Admiral Sir Barry Domville (bizarrely, Domville was incarcerated in Brixton prison in 1940 for three years on account of his extreme political views).[26] Boyle was promoted Admiral in 1932, followed by appointment as Commander in Chief of the Home Fleet. Two years later he succeeded his cousin as the 12th Earl of Cork and Orrery. His final appointment before retirement was as Commander in Chief Portsmouth during which time he was appointed Admiral of the Fleet. Although retired, he served in various naval posts in World War II, finally retiring from naval service in 1941.

He was a product of the Royal Navy of the late nineteenth century, with its methods and training. Proper and formal, among other training that young officers undertook he had passed through the disciplined training of HMS *Excellent*, the Navy's gunnery school at Whale Island, which was described earlier. His first meeting with TE Lawrence was not a success. He commented on the British officers who were arriving in Arabia in the summer and autumn of 1916, including, "lastly but by no means the least, TE Lawrence from the Arab Bureau in Cairo. Except Lawrence all these were officers of the Regular Army whom I could easily understand." Regular Army officers were out of the same mould as Boyle, with a background in the traditions and discipline of service life. Boyle commented that it had taken longer to appreciate Lawrence. He had met Lawrence earlier. At their first meeting on *Suva* on 1 November 1915, "[I] was a little astonished when a small, untidily dressed and most unmilitary figure strolled up to me on board the ship I was temporarily commanding and said, hands in pockets and so without a salute: 'I'm going over to Port Sudan in this ship'."

---

26. Which are explained in his book *From Admiral to Cabin Boy*.

Boyle was clearly deeply unimpressed: the ship's First Lieutenant, who witnessed the meeting said afterwards that he had "properly told off Captain Lawrence" for his lack of manners. A temporary army captain, well below a Captain of the Royal Navy, did not address such a person in that way! However, later, on frequent occasions he sailed as a passenger on HMS *Fox*, and Boyle came to appreciate his true worth.[27] Lawrence's memories of that first meeting reinforced its unfortunate nature: "It was not a good first meeting. I was travel-stained and had no baggage with me and on my head was a native head cloth."[28] He later described Boyle as "a very professional officer, as alert as any man could be, both businesslike and official, sometimes a little intolerant of easy-going things and people. Red haired men are seldom patient, and "Ginger Boyle", as the men called him was a warm man."[29]

Although it has been suggested that Boyle and Lawrence met in February 1915, when the landing at Alexandretta for a projected invasion of Syria was being researched by the Arab Bureau, it seems unlikely as Boyle, at that time, was the Naval Attaché in Rome.[30] Further, inspection of the Navy List has shown that, at the time, there were no other Captains with that surname.

The third officer to reach the rank of Admiral of the Fleet was the Commander in Chief of the East Indies Station, in overall command of the Red Sea Patrol. Vice Admiral Sir Rosslyn Wemyss took command in 1916. His flagship was the old four funnelled cruiser mentioned earlier, HMS *Euryalus*. He had, prior to that appointment, been in command of a squadron at Gallipoli, again on board *Euryalus*. As Commander in Chief, East Indies, his tactics in the Red Sea were successful, to the extent that after the war at the Versailles Peace Conference, General Botha of South Africa expressed to Emir Feisal his astonishment at the

---

27. *My Naval LIfe*, 99.
28. *Seven Pillars of Wisdom*, 97.
29. Ibid. 136.
30. *The Golden Warrior*, 46.

Arabs succeeding where the Boers had failed. The Emir replied, "That was because you had not Admiral Wemyss and his ships to help you."[31] Lawrence shared this high opinion:

> "Admiral Wemyss was in glorious contrast to the soldiers – no jealousy, no stupidity, no laziness; he was as keen to help as any two-year old ... he, with his active mind and broad intelligence, had taken the greatest interest in the Arab Revolt from the beginning. He had come down again and again in his flagship to lend a hand when things were critical and had gone out of his way 20 times to help them on shore, where properly it was the army's sphere ... Sir Rosslyn Wemyss acted Godfather till the Arabs were on their own feet."[32]

From Port Said he returned to London, to become First Sea Lord, in June 1917. In November 1918 he was one of Marshal Foch's guests to witness the signing of the Armistice. Promoted to Admiral in 1919, he retired in November of the same year, and was promoted to Admiral of the Fleet. He was also elevated to the peerage and took the title Baron Wester Wemyss.

The Navy's task

The Red Sea Patrol was initially divided into two sectors, the northern and southern, which operated to either side of the parallel of latitude 21° North. This passes about thirty miles south of Jeddah on the Arabian coast and about eighty miles north of Port Sudan on the African coast. This arrangement was made in 1915, with both sectors under the control of the then Commander-in-Chief, East Indies, Vice Admiral Sir R.F. Peirce KCB MVO, who was based at Port Said.

---

31. *Lord Wester Wemyss*, 358.
32. *Seven Pillars of Wisdom*, 98.

Although naval control was unified, the political control over the two areas was divided. The northern part was advised from Cairo by the Egyptian Government; the southern part was advised by the Indian Government's Political Resident who was based at Aden. The two authorities had differing views on various policies, which resulted in differing treatment being given to Arab dhows which were intercepted by Naval ships, depending on whether they were north or south of 21° North, which puzzled the Arab traders. This state of affairs continued until March 1916. The purpose of the two parts of the Patrol was to render a blockade, to prevent supplies from reaching Turkish troops. However, so as not to upset Muslim susceptibilities, no hostile action could be taken on the stretch of coast between Wejh and Jeddah. This area was known as the Holy territory, into which, before the war, no Christian was allowed to penetrate. To resolve the difficulties being caused by the geographical division of the Patrol, the new Commander in Chief, Vice Admiral Sir Rosslyn Wemyss, took two actions. He describes his policy:

"When I arrived out here in January [1916] I found the Red Sea Patrol divided into two distinct parts, one working politically under Egypt and the other politically under India, with no sort of liaison or cohesion between them. I saw at once that I had a chance of getting some sort of co-ordination between the two governments by amalgamating the two patrols into one, and I did this and actually got the Indian Government to borrow a political officer from Egypt to work on their behalf in their patrol! The results have more than justified my action, for I am quite sure that we never should have succeeded in getting India to assent to this Arabian policy."[33]

---

33. *The Life and Letters of Lord Wester Wemyss*, 317.

The Red Sea Patrol had had to act in a very circumspect manner because it was considered imprudent that it should be known that the Arabs were being supported by the British. This arose because the Turks had become the object of contempt by good Muslims, by allying themselves with Christians (in their case, the Germans). The Grand Sherif of Mecca had to be kept free from any similar taint. This policy caused those who were serving in that part of the world to agree with Lawrence's tag that they were part of "a sideshow of a sideshow". Their frustration must have been furthered by the policy of allowing food imports for the Arabs, whilst denying supplies to the Turks. As the Turkish authorities controlled the Customs and had garrisons at every port, this policy was not a great success. Additionally, the Indian Government sent supplies to Indian pilgrims who had been caught in Jeddah at the start of the war in British ships. The transfer of the cargoes into dhows, for landing, was undertaken under the supervision of Turkish officials which resulted in the supplies, unsurprisingly, not reaching their intended recipients. Other than at the ports and along the Hejaz railway, Turkish control of the country extended little further than rifle range from Turkish army posts, mainly along the railway and the garrisons stationed at Mecca and Medina. Control of the Hejaz was exercised in practice by the Grand Sherif, Emir Hussein; although appointed by the Turkish Sultan in 1908 and at that time residing in Constantinople he set out to acquire control over the Hejaz as the ultimate aim of gaining autonomy, or even independence. In this he was supported by his three elder sons, Ali, Abdullah and Feisal. His opposition to the extension of the Turkish built and operated Hejaz railway as far as Mecca won great favour with the Bedouin.

The tasks of the Red Sea Patrol were, firstly, to interdict the dhow traffic, which was the main means of transporting essential supplies to the various ports. Because of the length of the coast to watch – over 1,200 miles – no close blockade was possible with the number of ships available, so ships made visits to various ports and dismasted the dhows, removing their motive power. In Jeddah, for example, over

100 suffered this fate which both stopped the traffic and demonstrated to the Arabs the impotence of the Turks to prevent the damage. This tactic was more successful in the northern part of the Red Sea, but due to various political factors was less stringent in its application in the southern part. Secondly, in addition to this blockade, the ships also transported men, arms and supplies from Suez and Port Sudan to the Arabian coast and transported secret agents backwards and forwards.

The following chapters will describe how they achieved this.

Chapter Three

Build Up to the Revolt

HMS Northbrook

Formerly a Royal Indian Marine troop ship, converted to an auxiliary cruiser and commissioned into the Royal Navy.

T he work of the Red Sea Patrol had started when the Ottoman Empire declared war on the Allies on 29 October 1914. This caused Aqaba, the east coast of the Gulf of Aqaba and the east coast of the Red Sea to become enemy territory, past which, down the narrow width of that sea, went all the traffic sailing from or to the Suez Canal. At that time the British Merchant Navy flew its Red Ensign over half the world's merchant shipping. The fleets of P&O and British India Steam Navigation, amongst many others, maintained their links with India, Africa and the Far East, and interruption to this flow of traffic was clearly not something that the British Admiralty could countenance.

Turkey's Navy was led by two former German warships, the battle cruiser *Goeben* and the light cruiser *Breslau*. The offer of these ships had been, to a degree, conditional upon Turkey entering war as an ally of Germany. One of the factors in the acceptance of this offer was that Turkey had ordered two Dreadnought class battleships, similar to the Royal Navy's *Iron Duke* class, to be built by Vickers of Barrow. However, as the onset of war approached, both ships were still in the builder's yard, awaiting Turkish crews to sail them back to form the spearhead of the Turkish Navy. Winston Churchill, who by then was First Lord of the Admiralty, delayed the handover, until, on August 2, 1914, the ships were confiscated by the British Government and seized to join the British fleet, and renamed *Erin* (described in Jane's as follows: "Steams well, is a good sea-boat and remarkably handy") and *Agincourt* ("A good steamer, a good sea-boat and a steady gun platform").[1] The *Goeben* and the *Breslau* became the most modern units in the Turkish Navy.

In addition to the two warships provided by Germany, the Turkish Navy had two elderly cruisers, also built in Britain and comparable to the *Fox* in size and capability. The remainder of the Turkish fleet was comprised of small gunboats, a variety of transports and sundry smaller craft. David Gregory describes the Turkish Navy as "little more than a collection of unmanned, mouldering, obsolete hulks that had, for decades, been rotting at its moorings."[2]

The main base of the Turkish navy was at Istanbul; there was no naval base or any of the elements of the fleet located in the Red Sea. In order to reach there from Turkey, the most direct route is through the Suez Canal. Despite its international status under the Suez Canal Convention of 1888, which guaranteed the free passage of ships of

---

1. *"Jane's Fighting Ships of World War I"*,, 37 & 38.
2. *"The Lion and The Eagle"*, 402.

all nations "in war as in time of peace … The canal shall never be subjected to the exercise of the right of blockade",[3] the base of the Commander-in-Chief of the East Indies Station of the Royal Navy was located in Port Said, and British forces patrolled the canal. In practice it would have seemed unlikely that Turkey's warships, such as they were, would have been allowed to transit the Canal. The only other route for Turkish warships to reach the Red Sea would have been to pass through the Mediterranean, and round Africa. Given their condition, that also would not have happened. There was, therefore, effectively no Turkish naval resistance to the Red Sea Patrol.

Action against the Ottoman Empire's coast followed swiftly after her declaration of war on 29 October 1914. HMS *Minerva* had arrived in the Red Sea on 6 October and was engaged on patrols for the remainder of that month. At the beginning of November she was off to Aqaba to assess the Turkish strength there. Lieutenant Bruce Fraser, as he was then, was her gunnery officer. He was ordered to open fire on the Fort covering the approach to the port. Her 6-inch guns duly fired on target. Fraser commented later:

> "there was no reply, so we stopped; and the next thing that happened was a donkey, putting its head round the corner! This caused much hilarity throughout the ship."[4]

It was subsequently discovered, when a landing party was sent ashore, that Aqaba was unprotected by Turkish troops and mostly deserted. Because of its strategic position at the head of the Gulf of Aqaba it was to be regularly visited by other ships of the Red Sea Patrol. In itself it was singularly undistinguished. It is described by the Admiralty Pilot as:

---

3. *"The Sea and Civilisation"*, 526.
4. *Fraser of North Cape*, 35.

"a small Arab village, in an extensive date grove on the Eastern shore, nearly at the head of the Gulf. Close to the village is a small square Fort garrisoned by Turkish soldiers. This is a depot for grain for the use of caravans on their way to and from Mecca and a small supply of provisions may be obtained here … Near the Fort and in the adjacent country there are numerous ruins."[5]

After visits from other naval ships over the next year and a half, there were many more ruins.

Minerva continued to patrol off Aqaba for the next three months, visiting the port eight times, which produced a response from the Turks who infiltrated troops with light arms to snipe (ineffectually) at the patrolling ships and their landing parties. By this time *Minerva* was taking turns with the destroyers *Foxhound* and *Mosquito*, each ship lying off Aqaba for up to five days at a time. On 27 January she arrived at the Suez Canal as part of the naval force that was being assembled for the defence of the Canal. It had become clear in the middle of January that an attack on the Canal by Turkish forces was imminent. On the 18th, between 8,000 and 10,000 men were located by aerial reconnaissance near Beersheba, and other Turkish troops were subsequently encountered closer to the canal. As a result of these encroachments, eight warships, six from the Royal Navy and two from the French Navy, were stationed in the Canal to provide artillery support for the defence. Of the six ships of the Royal Navy, three were of the Red Sea Patrol. *Minerva* was already in the area; *Clio* had been on passage from the China station via Singapore and had arrived at Port Said in the middle of December where she had been stationed since then; the third ship was *Hardinge* which was already operating in the Red Sea.

The Turkish attacking force had approximately 25,000 men with nine batteries of Field Artillery and one battery of 5.9-inch howitzers. The

---

5. *Red Sea and Gulf of Aden Pilot*, 290.

canal was defended by a force of 70,000 troops, of which 25,000 were Indian, together with a total of ten batteries of light Field Artillery, to which were added the naval guns of the eight ships. The canal itself was patrolled by six Royal Navy torpedo boats together with tugs and launches of the Suez Canal Company. These were manned by Royal Navy personnel, armed with Maxim guns. Additional protection around the steering position and the boilers was provided against rifle fire.

The naval force built up from the third week of January. The *Clio*, which was moored at the entrance to the Suez Canal off Port Said, noted in her log on the 24th that the French ships *Requin* (a coastal defence ship, similar to a British monitor) and *d'Entrecasteaux* (an elderly cruiser, of the same vintage as *Fox* and *Minerva*) arrived at Port Said to take up station in the Canal. Two days later she herself entered the Canal, securing alongside the west bank south of Kantara, at Ballah Ferry. Advance parties of the Turkish army were spotted the next morning while her crew were employed filling sandbags and putting them in place as protection from rifle fire. At 1030 she fired on them with her 4-inch guns at extreme range, about five miles from the eastern bank of the Canal. In her position, little then happened until 1 February. Just after midday on that day she slipped her moorings and proceeded southwards, and at 1225 "opened fire on a reported force of 2000 Turks on a 370' hill SE of Katib Abu Azuk, but failed to locate them". Two hours later she moved further south to shell a position five miles north-east of Ismailia (on the eastern side of the canal). They located the enemy a mile west of the 370' hill but they were out of range. She ceased firing at 1515. On the next morning she opened fire just after 10 o'clock, on a body of Turkish troops which had been spotted north-east of Ismailia, at maximum range with her 4-inch guns. After 15 minutes she moved south and reopened fire until midday. Late in the afternoon, at 1735, she opened fire on enemy troops 5,000 yards east of the 66 km post, ceasing fire 25 minutes later. On 3 February, when the main attack took place, she opened fire at 0200 on a white light which had been seen about 800 yards away on the port beam, on the eastern side of the canal. An hour later, at 0300 the ship was fired on by enemy troops with rifles. After daylight, just before 0700, she opened fire with her port 4-inch guns, loaded with shrapnel shell on what appeared to be enemy trenches approximately 5,000 yards away. She then shifted her fire to a hilltop where there appeared to be enemy troops moving round a hut, although this proved to be just outside the range of her guns. The attack continued through the day. After 0900 enemy shrapnel fire fell on the El Fardan Post and the Canal buildings not far from *Clio*, so she moved over to the eastern bank and opened fire with her 4-inch guns to reply to this attack. The Turkish gunfire ceased at 1030; *Clio* ceased her own firing 10 minutes later. It was not only buildings that had been targeted; two hits on board were also noted, although there were no casualties. The enemy were seen retiring to the north-east with their guns, although soon after midday they reappeared about 6,000 yards away, and *Clio* re-engaged with her 4-inch guns until 1730. While she was firing, *Hardinge* passed going northwards and *Swiftsure* passed going southwards. The guns were silent for the rest of the day. During the early evening she moved north, securing alongside the canal north of El Fardan. Later in the evening she received a report that the enemy was digging trenches only 200 yards east of El Fardan, so she went to investigate, using her searchlights to cover the area where the enemy had been reported, but nothing was sighted and there was no return fire. Although she stayed in the area until 9 February there was no more action. On that day she sailed north to Port Said, stopping to talk with *Swiftsure* at Ismailia. She arrived at 1725, followed 2½ hours later by the *Hardinge*.

A week later she sailed for Bombay, from where, after a brief refit, she sailed to join the *Espiegle* on the Shatt al Arab in Mesopotamia.[6]

Minerva had arrived at Suez on 27 January, and taking a Canal pilot on board, sailed north up the Canal into the Big Bitter Lake (sic) where

---

6. An account of the *Clio*'s part in the defence of the Suez Canal, viewed through the experiences of one of her crew, is to be found in *Sailor in the Desert*.

there was space for her to turn, [7] then retraced her course back towards Suez before mooring at the southern end of Little Bitter Lake. The next day HMS *Himalaya,* an armed merchant cruiser (formerly a P&O liner), passed on her way north to take up her position as part of the naval defence.

A problem faced by the ships was the height of the sand dunes on the eastern bank near Lake Timsah, approximately halfway along the Canal. Ships moored there found that the banks were too high for their shells to clear even at extreme elevation. There were also difficulties for the gun layers who could not see over the banks, compounded by mirages in the desert.

The main attack started in the early hours of 3 February when the Turkish advance party reached the Canal near Tussum, where they launched rafts and pontoons into the Canal. This attack was engaged by machine gun fire from the Army and the machine guns of *Hardinge,* which was moored a little way to the south of the attack. Despite the machine gun fire, some of the Turkish troops succeeded in crossing, but were then charged by troops of the 62nd Punjabis with fixed bayonets. Those that were not killed were imprisoned; the remaining Turks on the eastern bank were fired on by *Hardinge* and *d'Entrecasteaux.* The effect of the naval support was to overwhelm the Turkish attack, which then retreated. A further attack at Kantara was repulsed and the Turkish forces retreated. The rate of retreat was accelerated by *Swiftsure's* [8] guns which kept firing whenever a target could be seen.

It was at this time that *Hardinge* came under fire. In the words of the official report:

---

7. The width of the canal was insufficient for ships of the size of *Minerva* to turn.
8. *Swiftsure,* with her sister ship *Triumph,* had been purchased from the Chilean Navy in 1903 whilst still building at British yards. A pre-Dreadnought battleship, she had 10-inch and 7.5-inch main guns.

"During the morning HMS *Hardinge* was struck by two 6 inch shells, her funnel being split and forward steering gear disabled. She moved to Lake Timsah and later to Kantara."[9]

Those are the words of the official report. The main attack by the Turkish army took place at Tussum, three miles north from where *Hardinge* was moored, at the southern end of Lake Timsah. She was providing artillery support, together with the *Requin* and *d'Entrecasteaux*, for four Indian battalions and other British units in that sector of the Canal. In that part, the banks of the Canal were some 50 feet high, which prevented *Hardinge* and the other ships from being able to fire on the Turkish attack. About 0700 she was fired on by 4-inch and 6-inch artillery, which because of the height of the banks she could neither locate nor reach to return fire. She therefore directed her fire at the troops which were visible in the open. She did manage to locate and silence a field gun battery at about 0815, but 10 minutes later she was hit by 6-inch shells, damaging both her funnels, and receiving other hits. One of the shells caused her Suez Canal pilot to receive severe injuries. George Carew, who had been a pilot in the Canal for twenty years, was hit:

"... his left leg was shattered by Turkish shrapnel and his arm broken. He also sustained grave head and back wounds. In spite of this he carried on on the bridge and brought the ship, still under fire, to safety and undoubtedly prevented a serious blockade of the Suez Canal at a most critical time. When he reached hospital eventually at Ismailia his case was considered hopeless. However his life was saved at the cost of the amputation of one of his legs. For this gallantry he was awarded the DSC and the [French] Legion of Honour, and was given the rank of Honorary Lieutenant in the Royal Navy."[10]

---

9. Despatch from Major General A. Wilson to Secretary of State for War 21 June 1915.
10. The Egyptian Gazette, "*Late Captain GJ Carew – An Appreciation*" 4th September 1936.

In any further communica-
tion on this subject, please quote

C.V. /M 17981

and address letter to—
The Secretary,
Admiralty, Whitehall,
London, S.W.

No

Admiralty,

8th April *19*15.

Sir,

      With reference to your submission of the 11th
February 1915, No 19/1077, I am commanded by My Lords Commissioners of the Admiralty to acquaint you that they have
been pleased to grant Mr George Carew a temporary commission
as Lieutenant in the Royal Naval Reserve from the 3rd
February 1915.

2.-   I am further to inform you that His Majesty has
been graciously pleased to award the Distinguished Service
Cross to this Officer, in recognition of his gallant conduct
on board on H.M.S."Hardinge" whilst in action at Toussoum
on 3rd February 1915.

3.-   A further communication will be made as regards the
compensation Lieutenant Carew R.N.R. will receive.

4.-   His commission is forwarded herewith.

      I am, Sir,

      Your obedient Servant,

W Graham Greene

The Commander in Chief,
  H.M.Ships and Vessels,
    East Indies.

He was also the subject of a report in the French Press after he was awarded the Legion d'Honneur.

A letter from the Admiralty dated 8 April 1915, to Commander in Chief East Indies, gives George Carew's correct rank:

"Sir

1. With reference to your submission of 11 February 1915, Reference Number 19/1077, I am commanded by my Lords Commissioners of the Admiralty to acquaint you that they have been pleased to grant Mr George Carew a temporary commission in the Royal Naval Reserve from 3 February 1915.

2. I am further to inform you that His Majesty has been graciously pleased to award the Distinguished Service Cross to this Officer in recognition of his gallant conduct aboard HMS *Hardinge* whilst in action at Toussom on the 3 February 1915.

3. A further communication will be made as regards the compensation Lieutenant Carew RNR will receive.

4. His commission is forwarded herewith.

I am, Sir, Your Obedient Servant

W Graham Greene."[11]

In order for George Carew, a civilian, to be awarded the DSC for gallantry, he first had to be given a temporary commission in the Royal Naval Reserve, as civilians were ineligible for gallantry awards. This was also the practice for Merchant Service officers who had performed actions of gallantry, in order that their bravery could be recognised.

George Carew had not been the only casualty on the *Hardinge*. Austin Christian, ranked Boy, First-Class (so, by definition, under 18) died of his wounds. Albert Rust, also Boy, First Class was dangerously wounded and died of his wounds six days later. His family had been

---

11. Letter in the possession of Captain JRJ Carew OBE RFA (grandson of George Carew).

advised of his wounds very quickly; his mother had written to the Admiralty on 5 February, only two days after he was hit asking where he was and as to his condition. No reply having been received, Albert's former headmaster wrote to the Admiralty on the ninth, on behalf of his parents asking once again where he was in hospital and what his injuries were. He died three days after the date of that letter.

Minerva had, after arriving at her position at the southern end of the Little Bitter Lake, had an incident-free time until the third, when the main attacks were happening further north. On that morning she slipped her moorings and sailed south. After about an hour Turkish cavalry was sighted on the east bank and one of her 12-pounder guns fired five rounds. The results of this were not noted in her log. She continued on her way, out of the Canal before turning and re-entering the Canal mooring just inside the entrance. She stayed at Suez, taking on 200 tons of bunker coal. After that was completed, the log notes "hands employed washing down", the hands washing away the coal dust that had settled on the ship. Whilst still moored, the next day a passing British merchant ship, SS *City of Poona*, collided with her tearing off a length of *Minerva*'s handrails and damaging one of the *City of Poona*'s lifeboats. It was noted that this had occurred because she was passing very slowly and therefore did not have enough steerage way to keep a straight course.

She remained in the Canal until 10 February, when she boarded a battalion of the 2/7th Gurkhas, under the command of Colonel Haldane, for landing at Tor, on the eastern side of the Gulf of Suez on the Sinai peninsula. Tor is a small harbour, which:

> "... is not sufficiently roomy for very large vessels, nor for the number of smaller vessels by which it is sometimes filled during the pilgrim season. The old town stands at the northern end of the harbour and has some well-built stone houses, a large Greek church and a garden with good water. Southward of the old town is a Fort ... in ruins. Communication is maintained with Suez by

overland telegraph wire and with the monastery at Mount Sinai by means of camels."[12]

At Tor there was a manganese mine which was under threat of a Turkish attack. The offensive by the Gurkhas was a considerable success; for the loss of one killed and one wounded, 60 Turks were killed and a further 102 captured. Returning the Gurkhas to Suez, *Minerva* sailed south and joined *Fox* and *Northbrook* at the end of March, when the Commander in Chief, on board *Euryalus*, arrived at Aden.

Dufferin, which was at Suez at the end of January, rather than joining the defence of the Suez Canal, was sent down the Gulf of Suez to Tor, where she arrived on the 30th. She stayed there at anchor, sporadically firing at Turkish patrols until *Minerva* arrived on the 11th, when she sent all her boats over to assist with the landing of the Gurkhas. She stayed until the action was over when she assisted with the re-embarkation of troops, before returning to Suez to take on coal, and then returned to Tor.

After *Hardinge*'s action in the Suez Canal, there is no further news of her until 1 April; the logs for that period are missing. The necessary repairs were clearly undertaken, probably in Port Said where she had arrived on 9 February, because on 1 April she was in Tor, and was patrolling, with a complete lack of incident for that month and for the following month in the Northern Red Sea. However, at the beginning of June she was in Suez where she hoisted on board a French seaplane, embarking a French pilot to fly it. She sailed to Mowila where, two days later, the seaplane was hoisted out. It took off just before 0800 and returned one and a quarter hours later. The seaplanes remained on board for the month of June and were operated in various places. Her pattern of patrolling in the Gulf of Suez carried on in July; in the middle of the month she was anchored off Hassani Island for three days, noting in her log on the 17th that one Able Seaman and

---

12. *Red Sea and Gulf of Aden Pilot*, 104.

one Royal Marine Light Infantry private, of one of the ship's cutters, who had been placed in charge of a dhow had failed to return to the ship by 2200. There was no further note in the log, so they most likely returned safely at some stage. Clearly there was not much to keep the *Hardinge* active; she returned to Hassani Island and anchored on the 22nd remaining there until 2 August when she sailed for Suez, where she moored in one of the Suez Canal berths and remained there until 13 November. The stay was without incident except when, on 13 October, the *Dufferin* was passing and collided with *Hardinge* causing a significant amount of damage. The list, quoted in full in *Hardinge*'s log, includes one 28-foot cutter, with its compass, signal book, white Ensign, answering pennant and boat hook which were all lost. The impact of the collision also broke 155 pieces of crockery or glass. The damage to the ship's side and railings is not noted, but an impact of that force would undoubtedly have had a noticeable effect.

Wemyss had welcomed the news that the Arabs had taken possession of Mecca and Jeddah and driven out the Turks. "Now I flatter myself that this is a result, at any rate indirectly, of my policy. It was always the policy to try and get the Arabs to rise against the Turks, but India would not face the situation. Why I cannot imagine, because it appears to me that Mecca in the hands of friendly Arabs, who moreover are much more orthodox and strict Mahommedans than the Turks, must act favourably on the Mahommedans of India and Egypt. When I arrived out here in January I found the Red Sea Patrol divided into two distinct parts, one working politically under Egypt and the other politically under India with no sort of liaison or cohesion between them. I saw at once that I had a chance of getting some sort of coordination between the two Governments in the matter of policy by amalgamating the two patrols into one, and I did this and actually got the Indian Government to borrow a political officer from Egypt to work on their behalf in their patrol! The results have more than justified my action, for I am quite sure that three months ago we should never have succeeded in getting India to assent to this Arabian policy. This should enormously ease matters in the East … at Aden too the difficulties of the Turks will be very much augmented, and I should think the effects should reach as far as Syria. Boyle, late naval attaché in Rome is my Senior Officer in the Red Sea and he is doing splendidly."[13]

The Naval Review also, in a somewhat more measured manner, explained the policies of Cairo and Bombay in relation to the treatment of shipping in the northern and southern part of the Red Sea:

"Politically the Northern Patrol was advised from Cairo, while the Southern carried out the policy of the Indian government as made known through the Political Resident at Aden. As the policies of these two authorities are not always working in the same direction, a somewhat anomalous state of affairs resulted and a different treatment was meted out to dhows according as to whether they were north or south of latitude 21° N. To the Arab traders this was perplexing.[14] The general policy was one which aimed at conciliating the Arabs by keeping up hostilities against the Turks. With this in view, food etc, was allowed to be imported for Arab consumption but cargoes were to be destroyed if supposed to be destined for the Turks. When it is stated that the Turks controlled the customs and had garrisons at every port, the success that this policy achieved can be estimated. Moreover, British steamers laden with foodstuffs were sent to Jeddah by the Indian Government, and these cargoes were checked into dhows by enemy officials. The food thus imported was supposed to be for certain Indian pilgrims caught in Jeddah on the outbreak of war. In practice it was a free gift to the Turks. The general situation was from a naval point of view most unsatisfactory."[15]

---

13. *Wester Wemyss*, 317.
14. Dhows did not navigate by reference to lines of latitude – the concept would have been unknown to them.
15. *Naval Operations in the Red Sea, 1916–17.*

In the southern part of the Red Sea, patrols were also taking place in 1915. *Northbrook*, *Minto* and *Lama* were based in Aden covering the area south of 21° North. The Arabian coastline patrolled by the ships based at Aden fell into two parts: the Asir, immediately south of the Hejaz, and the Yemen, which is between Asir and the Aden Protectorate. The latter was under British control. The coast of the Yemen was, in general, controlled by the Turks, who maintained garrisons at Loheia (which was dismissed by the Red Sea Pilot as "a collection of miserable looking straw huts"[16]), Salif, Hodeidah and Mocha, the four main ports of the region. Opposite Salif is the island of Kameran which was occupied in early 1915 by a garrison of Indian troops. Asir was partly ruled by the Idrissi, who was unofficially recognised by the Turks, whose influence was exercised over the small port of Qunfunda.

The main part of their work was the normal fare of the blockading patrol; checking craft for cargoes and intercepting ships of foreign flags. On 27 April, *Northbrook* received passengers (whose names and purposes were not specified in her log) and mail from the SS *Empress of Japan*, a British passenger liner. Later that day, she stopped and boarded an Italian ship, SS *Massawa*. However, it was the interdiction of the dhow traffic which was the most important, as they did not carry only stores. On 15 May a dhow was stopped and searched and found to contain sixteen German passengers as well as stores. Both the Germans and the dhow's crew were taken prisoner. More Germans were found on the last day of May, when off Perim, at the very southern end of the Red Sea – a Swedish ship, SS *Canton* was stopped and searched. Fourteen Germans were found on board and taken prisoner. The ships of the southern part of the Red Sea Patrol continued their patrols from Aden for the remainder of 1915 without significant excitement.

---

16. *Red Sea and Gulf of Aden Pilot*, 359.

Chapter Four

The Arrival of William Boyle:
September 1915–June 1916

HMS Espiegle

"Is far smaller than the classic Channel boats without even
any of their basic amenities" *(Storrs)*

In September 1915, Captain Boyle at last had his wish and left his
post as Naval Attaché at Rome. After the war had started, Boyle
had become increasingly frustrated at being stuck in a backwater.
"I could not face a second winter of comparative idleness in Rome."
He took his troubles to the ambassador:

"what he did was to write privately to Mr Balfour who had just become First Lord of the Admiralty. He did not tell me what he had said, but ... he mentions (in his book) that he obtained the release of the Naval Attaché 'who was in a condition bordering on melancholia at being chained to a desk in wartime'."[1]

He left, without having to await his relief, to take command of HMS *Fox*. After meeting the Commander in Chief in Port Said he was told,

"that his policy was do everything that the Army asked him to do but not to take the initiative in any way. I was warned that as I was going down the Red Sea I was to remember this and to act accordingly."[2]

He proceeded to Suez to join his ship; as she was awaiting a new crew he had to wait a week for them to arrive. When he joined her, the Red Sea Patrol was still under the command of Sir Richard Peirce, who he had recently met in Port Said, and divided into two parts. His immediate superior was therefore Rear Admiral Huguet, of the French Navy, through his flag in the cruiser *Montcalm*. Boyle only met him once, before he returned to France in December.

On his first cruise Boyle also went to Aqaba, on 30 January 1916, where the *Fox*'s 4.7-inch guns fired on a blockhouse, and subsequently landed an armed party from the ship's cutter. Turkish troops were in position, who returned fire without effect on the ship or the armed party. The earlier attacks on Aqaba were evident, as he described the town of Aqaba as being "a collection of hovels into which several ships had fired on some excuse or other, generally saying that they had done so to destroy Government buildings, though it would have been

---

1. *My Naval Life*, 94.
2. Ibid. 95.

quite impossible to distinguish one such building from the ordinary houses."[3]

The entry to the Gulf of Aqaba was through the Tiran Strait, which was a particularly dangerous piece of water, so much so that ships of the Red Sea Patrol when passing through it would close all watertight doors throughout the ship because of the proximity of the reefs. The Red Sea Pilot makes it very clear:

"The entrance to the Gulf of Aqaba is nearly closed by the island of Tiran with its extensive reefs. The Strait of Tiran is the passage on the western side of that island; it is 4 miles wide and there are depths of 70 fathoms within a mile of Ras Nuzeraini on the western side of the entrance. Reefs project west from Tiran island towards the coast reef, extending five cables from Ras Nuzeraini, leaving a channel only about two cables [less than a quarter of a mile] wide between the edges of these dangers through the Straits. Through this channel the wind and swell come down with great force at times."

Because of the slow speed of some of the ships, these dangers were very real.

At the same time that patrols were being undertaken up and down the Red Sea in 1915, the idea of an Arab rebellion against the Ottoman government was being discussed in a series of letters between the British High Commissioner in Egypt, Sir Henry McMahon, and the Emir of Mecca, Sherif Hussein bin Ali. Although these letters were later at the root of the controversy over Britain's promises with regard to the formation of an independent Arabia, at the time it encouraged the onset of the Arab revolt.[4] The series of letters was passed through the hands of Ronald Storrs, the Oriental Secretary of the Egyptian

---

3. Ibid. 96.

4. *A History of the Modern Middle East*, 158.

government, who commented later that, in his opinion "the Sharif opened his mouth and the British Government their purse a good deal too wide".[5] In his view there was "little agreement between the views of the Foreign Office, the India Office, the Admiralty, the War Office, the Government of India and the British Residency in Egypt".[6] However, a date was agreed for the start of the Arab revolt: 9 June 1916.

At the beginning of January 1916 *Dufferin* was in Bombay, from where she sailed on 11 January for Aden, arriving in Port Sudan on the 20th; *Hardinge* was proceeding from Tor to Aden, from where she was proceeding to Bombay for dry dock; *Northbrook, Minto* and *Lama* were still in the Southern Red Sea; and *Fox* was in Port Sudan, preparing to sail to Jeddah, which she did on the 3rd. *Minerva*, as we have seen, was patrolling in the Northern Red Sea. *Espiegle* had not yet joined the Red Sea Patrol, and was operating in the Persian Gulf. By the middle of January, *Dufferin* had completed her dry docking and had returned to Aden, where Commander Warren took over command. The following day she sailed for Port Sudan, from where, on the 23rd, she commenced patrolling in the northern sector. *Fox* was also patrolling. On the 26th, her log notes that she was anchored off Hassani Island and, at 1645, "landed fire engine to put out fire in tomb". The cause of the fire and the success of the fire fighting operation were not, regrettably, noted. The anchorage at Hassani Island was popular with ships of the Red Sea Patrol.

> "It is about 9 miles to the mainland which here forms a deep bay in which are several reefs, and two small islets, Maliha and Umm Sahr ... There is spacious anchorage near the South East end of Hassani Island in depths [from] 10–15 fathoms ... The best anchorage is under the East side of the island, close to a large Arab village inhabited for some months in the year by people

---

5. Ronald Storrs, *Orientations*, 153.

6. Ibid, 154.

from the mainland. This anchorage affords shelter from all winds."[7]

At the end of the month, described above, she went to Aqaba continuing her patrol before coaling in Suez on 6 February.

A particular feature of the *Dufferin*'s log was the regularity of breakages of crockery and glassware reported. On the 20 January, her log notes that tea cups and saucers, coffee cups, plates, butter dishes and hot water jugs were all broken because of the weather. The weather on that occasion was force six to seven, near gale force, and the sea state was noted as six – rough. *Dufferin* was however not a small ship, and her crew were experienced and should have ensured that breakables were secure in the event of bad weather. Further losses were noted, whilst in port in Suez at the beginning of February, when two blankets were lost while the bedding was being aired. The log at the time recorded that the wind was only force two on the Beaufort scale – scarcely enough to lose blankets being aired. (It was remarked: "native crew"). Breakages continued: "crockery broken by rolling of ship", "ship pitching and rolling, shipping water forward". On this occasion the wind was from the south-east, force four, which is no more than a steady breeze and makes the movement of the ship sufficient to break crockery somewhat surprising.

On 14 February, back at Suez, *Dufferin* embarked over 200 Sikh troops which she took to, and disembarked the same evening at, Abu Zenima. She then embarked 150 Egyptian troops which she then took to Tor, also in the Gulf of Suez, on the Sinai Peninsula.

Seven days later, when *Fox* was on her way again to Hassani Island she hoisted the Russian Ensign and fired a twenty-one gun salute. This coincided with the opening of the Duma, in Petrograd (now St Petersburg) by the Emperor, for the first time in its history. On the last day of February, the 29th (being a leap year), she revisited Aqaba.

---

7. *Red Sea and Gulf of Aden Pilo*, 305.

Sending landing parties ashore in her boats, they were fired upon by Turkish forces, so fire was returned by her 4.7-inch guns, to allow the landing party to withdraw. After two block houses were destroyed, a further landing party went ashore to attack Turkish positions, under the shelter of shrapnel shells fired from the *Fox*'s 6-inch guns. She sailed the next day, patrolling for a further two days, and then arrived in Suez on 3 March to coal ship. On the 12th *Suva* arrived, and noted in her log that in addition to *Fox* and *Minerva* of the Patrol there were several other Navy ships present, including *Glory*, an elderly battleship; Jane's had said of her and her sister ships in 1914 that they "are getting worn out and few can now steam well except for short spurts".[8] *Jupiter*, another battleship of the same vintage and type, and *Ben-my-Chree* had also arrived that day.

No action had been taken up to that time on the part of the coast in the northern part of the Red Sea known as the holy coast, in the area of Jeddah and Medina, but this changed in March. In the ongoing series of letters between McMahon and Sherif Hussein, the latter wrote in March asking the British to blockade the Hejaz coast in the hope that this would be blamed on the presence of the Turks in the area and turn the pro-Turkish factions in Jeddah to support Hussein.[9]

As a result, *Fox* sailed from Suez en route for Port Sudan on the 13th. From there she sailed further down the Red Sea, stopping off at Yenbo, and then anchoring off the East coast of Hassani Island. She weighed anchor on the morning of the 21st and, steaming nine miles east, arrived off Umm Lejh just before 1000. Opening fire within ten minutes, her gunfire destroyed the custom house and a fort; after bombarding those targets for half an hour she turned her guns on a trench and the, by then retreating, Turks. Simultaneously, her steam cutter, armed with a Maxim machine gun, was also firing on the Turks. As a result, a Turkish officer and twelve men were killed. *Suva*, on the

8. *Jane's Fighting Ships 1914*, 53.
9. James Barr, *Setting the Desert on Fire*, 23.

same day, was also in action at Wejh, approximately ninety miles north, bombarding a fort. She had stopped off at Wejh at 0845, opening fire three quarters of an hour later. Firing ceased after thirty minutes; her log noted, "Secure. [i.e. cease fire] Fort observed to be in ruins." She was on her way two minutes later. The Naval Review commented: "Turkish truculence on the coast ceased." After bombarding Umm Lej, *Fox* returned to Hassani Island, from where she sailed to Jeddah, taking the opportunity to fire at a dhow off the town on the 25th.

The *Dufferin* had returned to Suez arriving on the 28th. An important passenger boarded on 30 March when the Prince of Wales came on board with his staff, to take passage to Port Sudan. He was going to inspect British troops stationed there, that were part of the regiments of which he was the Colonel.

There is a box in each day's log in which provisions and stores taken on board are recorded. There was no note prior to the Prince of Wales' passage on the ship of any special food being provided, so it must be assumed that he ate the standard fare of the ship's officers, which would undoubtedly have included curry at least once a day, prepared by the ship's Indian cooks. Standards on the Royal Indian Marine ships for the officers were very high. Storrs noted, when invited by Captain Turton to breakfast on the *Northbrook*:

"a floating Ritz ... Spotless napery etc., and neat handed [Goanese] stewards and the classical Breakfast of the English Gentleman in a luxurious carpeted enclosure on the upper deck."[10]

The Prince of Wales would have been well cared for.

On the same day that *Dufferin* was receiving her important passenger, *Fox* arrived at Aden, where *Minerva*, *Northbrook* and Admiral Wemyss' flagship, *Euryalus* were already moored. This gathering of ships was for the conference, called by Wemyss, at which he abolished the divided

---

10. *Orientations*, 180.

control of the Red Sea Patrol, joining the ships into one unit, and making Captain Boyle of the *Fox* the Senior Naval Officer. He also brought together representatives of the Egyptian and Indian governments and the Navy, to arrive at a better and united outcome. The conference agreed that the blockade of the coast would be made as effective as possible, given the limitations of the number of ships and the size of the patrol area. To that end, necessary warnings were to be sent out to all who would be affected by this policy. Thus, the first move of the united patrol would be to visit all the ports and force the dhows that were there to beach themselves. They would then be dismasted, to prevent their further use. At Jeddah over 100 dhows were dismasted in this way. As well as stopping the traffic of dhows up and down the coast, this policy also showed the Arabs that the Turks were powerless to protect them.[11]

Wemyss subsequently noted,

"meanwhile I have arranged the blockade on Jeddah and the way is open to the pilgrims for the first time since the war began. Of course we cannot help the Sherif of Mecca with Christian troops – it is part of our bargain and naturally the true policy that no unbelievers shall enter the Holy Region. Personally I am inclined to think that the Sherif has bitten off more than he can swallow and that we shall probably hear of Mecca falling into the hands of the Turks again before long. But in the meantime I have the Red Sea properly in my hands and have completely put a stop to any enemy traffic there. I shall of course see the High Commissioner and all his people before very long and shall hear their views. People who know the Mahommedan world well tell me that there is always a danger of a fanatical wave passing over it *suddenly* – but if no action takes place immediately after a crisis, there is little danger of such happening afterwards ..."[12]

---

11. *Naval Operations in the Red Sea 1916–17*, 653.
12. *Wester Wemyss*, 321.

The conference over, *Fox* sailed for Port Sudan on 3 May, the day that *Dufferin* had arrived there with the Prince of Wales, who, with his staff, disembarked to inspect the troops. The garrison of troops at Port Sudan followed the establishment of the port after its selection, in 1906, as the terminus of the Sudan and Red Sea railway, which connected it with Khartoum. It had embarked on a rapid state of development to become one of the principal ports in the Red Sea, including the construction of quays which were fitted with electric cranes for loading cargo.

The *Espiegle* had sailed from Muscat, returning from her action in the Mesopotamian rivers, and arrived at Aden, also on the 3rd. She sailed two days later, and then took a week to reach Suez, at her best speed of about 7½ knots. She passed through the Canal to Port Said, where her crew was changed and she re-commissioned with a new Commanding Officer, Commander Betts. Apart from a foray to Famagusta, in Cyprus, she paid little part in the ensuing events. Apart from two days in May, she spent her time alongside at Port Said until the middle of September. *Fox* also was at Suez, in dry dock for ten days. *Dufferin* continued her patrolling activities, along with *Suva*. On Sunday 5th, the latter was in the Gulf of Aqaba where, after divisions and morning prayers at 0900, she arrived off Aqaba at 1100, and opened fire, destroying some earthworks. Thirty minutes later she proceeded on her way, resuming her patrol back into the Red Sea. *Dufferin* continued to lose crockery broken by the "rolling of the ship".

Before the attacks on Umm Lejh and Wejh, following the request from Hussein to blockade the Hejaz coast, on 1 May "5,000 Japanese rifles and over two million rounds of ammunition were shipped to the Hejaz", and the smuggling of large quantities of gold also began.[13] How this was transported, it has not been possible to discover. The logs of the ships of the Red Sea Patrol show that none of them were in the Northern Red Sea at the beginning of May and none were noted loading guns, ammunition or gold (or, as it was referred to in

---

13. *Setting the Desert on Fire*, 23.

the logs, "specie"). Cargoes of that sort were noted on other dates; and there was no evidence of the logs being altered or rewritten. It is possible, however, that the armaments and gold could have been carried by one of the ships of the Khedivial Mail Line Company which was formed in 1898 to operate ships and other assets owned by the Egyptian government. The fleet was registered under the British flag and operated passenger and cargo services between Suez and the Red Sea ports. Two of the ships, *Borolus* and *Mansoura*, are mentioned by TE Lawrence, and it is possible, as part of the fleet that operated in the Red Sea, that they were used for this purpose, to be less noticeable than a British warship.

The pressure on the Arabian coast continued. On the 13th *Fox* arrived at Loheiya, from the anchorage at Kameran Island, at the southern end of the Red Sea, where she had been for two days with the *Minto* on exercises. Sailing from Kameran she arrived four hours later; an armed launch also called "*Kameran*", which had a small crew commanded by a Chief Petty Officer, arrived with two smaller boats shortly after 1600 and immediately started a search of the coast to the north. These patrols continued, successfully driving ashore a dhow and a sambuk, both of which were carrying contraband. On the 17th a skiff with a crew commanded by Lt Thompson RNR was launched in the depth of night to reconnoitre close inshore, but was detected and fired upon by shore batteries. Later in the day, *Fox* opened fire with her 6-inch and 4.7-inch guns on the town's customhouse. Fire was returned from the shore batteries, the Turks firing shrapnel; *Fox's* 4.7-inch guns silenced the shore battery. Two days later *Northbrook* and *Lama* arrived in the afternoon, the former sailing after two hours, followed by the *Fox* an hour later.

At the same time as the *Fox* and *Kamaran* were at Loheiya, *Hardinge* arrived at Jeddah. Her arrival caused uproar and the Turkish commander in Mecca was ordered to reinforce Jeddah from the small force that he commanded. Anchoring just before 1000 she deployed her boats to enforce a blockade of the port, checking dhows and confiscating cargo; by the 21st she had taken on board over 6,000 bags of contraband stores. The blockade continued through the days and nights that followed. She remained there until *Fox* arrived on 1 June; then *Hardinge* sailed to Port Sudan, discharged the cargo from Jeddah and loaded cased petroleum. Returning to Jeddah on the 4th, she discharged this into a dhow the following day. After a foray to Sherm Ubber, where her boats, led by the steam cutter, carried out a sweep for more dhows, she returned to Jeddah to rejoin *Fox* the next day.

On the 28th May Ronald Storrs joined *Dufferin*, which was by then at Suez. He was accompanied by Lieutenant Commander Hogarth RNVR[14] and Captain Cornwallis, both from the Arab Bureau in Cairo. They carried with them £10,000 in gold (approximately £400,000 in today's values), escorted for safety's sake by two NCOs. They sailed the following morning and met *Fox* two days later off Port Sudan. The *Fox* had carried Storrs' agent Ruhi, who updated Storrs as to the current situation. After taking Storrs to various localities to meet political agents of the Sherif, they arrived at Jeddah on 5 June. He described it as "a fine town with four and even five-storey houses and one minaret nearly as much out of the perpendicular as the leaning Tower of Pisa".[15] A meeting with Hussein's youngest son Zeid and Emir Shahir of the Ateibah tribe had been arranged, as Abdullah, his elder brother, was otherwise engaged. On the morning of the sixth, *Dufferin* sailed to Somerin, a little way from Jeddah, arriving at daybreak. Storrs was taken to the shore in the ship's cutter, towed by her steam launch from a position some two miles offshore. He was accompanied by Hogarth, Cornwallis, two of the Sherif's agents, the £10,000 in gold and two sacks containing copies of the Arab propaganda newspaper for distribution. As Zeid had not arrived they waited on a dhow, shaded from the sun,

14. Hogarth was the Curator of the Ashmolean Museum in Oxford before the war, and was a mentor of Lawrence.
15. *Orientations*, 156.

until he did. Storrs went to meet him on his own, travelling the last short distance to the beach in an Arab canoe, which had enough water in it to force him to stand. He was carried the last thirty yards by two slaves, who succeeded in soaking him, in his white suit, to well above his knees. In this somewhat undignified way, for a British diplomat representing the British High Commissioner, he met Zeid.

Storrs noted that Zeid was "the younger son of the Sharif by his second wife, a Circassian of good family, is, and looks, about 20 years of age ... At first he seemed a little shy and perhaps a little suspicious."[16] They had a meeting ashore of over an hour. In the course of that meeting Zeid handed over various documents the first of which contained a request for a total of £70,000. After the meeting Storrs then persuaded Zeid that he should visit *Dufferin*, to take breakfast on board. Picking up Hogarth and Cornwallis from the dhow they returned on board for further discussion in which Boyle joined, from *Fox*, which had also arrived. They were also shown round the ship, including the wireless office, the guns and the Captain's bathroom (presumably in the absence of the Captain). After about three hours of discussions, Zeid and Shahir left, carrying with them the £10,000, the propaganda newspapers and a thousand cigarettes as a gift for Feisal and Ali.

Hogarth's view of the situation, after the meeting, was that the forthcoming revolt was inadequately prepared; the Arabs had no knowledge of modern warfare and that the Sherif and his sons had little idea of the obligations it would place upon them.[17]

The date for the start of the Revolt had been agreed as 9 June at 2100. Unsurprisingly, this had become widely known and, at least inland in Taif, near Mecca, rumours of the impending uprising had caused many to pack and leave the town.

---

16. Ibid. 158.
17. "Middle East Politics and Diplomacy 1904–56", www.adammatthewpublications.co.uk.

Jeddah had some drawbacks as a port for the Navy to use. The entrance to the harbour, although marked by buoys and beacons, was difficult because "reliance cannot be placed on beacons or buoys in Jeddah harbour, as the former are often destroyed, and the latter break adrift and there is much delay in rebuilding and replacing them. Towards noon is the best time for entering, as owing to the clearness of the water, the sunken rocks then appear as a dark green shadow on the surface, but when the sun is low to the eastward and there is much glare, or in thick, greasy or cloudy weather the rocks cannot be discovered until close upon them. Much care is required in long vessels entering or leaving the port, as the turnings being sharp, such vessels are much more liable to take the ground than shorter ones."[18] *Fox, Dufferin*, and *Hardinge* definitely were in the category of "long vessels". The Pilot goes on to describe the town:

"Jeddah is the port of Mecca … and is in the province of Hejaz …
The town, with its white minarets has an imposing appearance from sea; it is half a mile square and enclosed by a wall, with small towers at intervals, the angles towards the sea being commanded by two forts. In the Northern Fort is the prison …
On the northern side of the town are several old windmills and near them a large tomb, said to be that of Eve. The streets are very narrow and irregular; the houses are mostly constructed of coralline limestone and some of the newest are large and well built. The population is estimated at about 20,000."[19]

As well as native Arabs, there was also a large number of Hindustani Indians. Every year 50,000 to 60,000 pilgrims arrived at Jeddah, many of them from India and the port. Although it had no jetties or wharves, it was served by up to twelve different shipping lines.

---

18. *Red Sea and Gulf of Aden Pilot*, 328.
19. *Red Sea and Gulf of Aden Pilot*, 329.

The *Fox* had arrived off Jeddah on 1 June and anchored at 1850; the *Hardinge* arrived a week later, after loading cargo and ammunition the previous day in Port Sudan. All was set for the start of the Arab Revolt.

Chapter Five

The Start of the Revolt:
9 June 1916–30 September 1916

HMS Dufferin

A near sister to *Northbrook* and *Hardinge*, she carried horses, camels, stores,
ammunition, and helped to rebuild the port of Rabegh.

A t 2100 on Friday 9 June, three hours before the end of the
Muslim holy day, *Fox* and *Hardinge*, both anchored in position
ready off Jeddah, switched on their searchlights to illuminate
the tall white buildings that Storrs had mentioned.[1] Both opened fire
together. The Turks had been well aware of the forthcoming attack
as they had spent the day raising defences against an Arab attack
from the land. An attack from the sea had been anticipated and all

---

1. In 1961 the author, in a ship anchored off Mukalla, in the Gulf of Aden, saw an
   identical site: four and five story white buildings shining in the glare of the summer
   sun.

the defences against seaborne attack were ready. Even if some of the Turkish troops may have experienced searchlights and naval gunfire, the effect on the majority of the Arab population of their town being lit up by searchlights from the sea and the shelling from large naval artillery close offshore, would have been akin to the "shock and awe" attacks on Baghdad in the next century.

Fox and *Hardinge* kept up the bombardment for two hours, firing on Turkish trenches to the northern end of the town, causing crockery on *Hardinge* to be broken during the bombardment. They ceased fire at 2300, only to resume the next day at 0830. The bombardment continued throughout the day, although the *Hardinge* ceased fire at 1130 until 1430, as the log notes "for dinner". The bombardment then continued until 2300. The next day, Sunday, the bombardment was restricted to an hour by the *Fox* in the late afternoon, to allow the crew some rest and relaxation. However, on Monday morning, *Fox* observed an Arab attack on Turkish positions, so the *Hardinge* opened fire at 0500 followed by the *Fox* at 0630. Boyle, on *Fox*, had found a local sheik to point out suitable targets, as Sherif Ali, in charge of the Arab forces, refused to allow naval observers to land to observe the fall of shot as, he claimed, it was holy ground. Boyle's sheik turned out to be a local merchant, who was ensuring that the buildings of his rivals were destroyed, instead of valid military targets. Boyle was not impressed by the Arabs:

> "They were difficult to work with; they would not allow us to establish observation posts on shore; they failed to carry out arrangements previously made and had no idea of time. The only attempt at assault was started two hours before the ships had been asked to open fire and by the time they were ready to do so the attack had collapsed and the plain was full of flying Arabs pursued by Turkish shrapnel."[2]

---

2. *My Naval Life*, 97.

Despite the prohibition by Sherif Ali on the landing of naval officers, *Fox* landed her Medical Officer and a support party to help the Arab wounded.

Dufferin arrived on the 13th and joined in the bombardment, followed the next day by *Perth,* and from 1630 on that day all four ships were bombarding the town.

On the following day the seaplane carrier *Ben-my-Chree* arrived. She had sailed from Perim, en route for Port Sudan to take on coal, but was diverted to Jeddah. After conferring with Boyle, seaplanes SP850, SP3790 and SP3789 were lifted out and launched into the waters of the harbour, in the late afternoon, from where they took off in ideal conditions from a calm sea and with a light wind. They proceeded to bomb and machine gun Turkish positions. One of the planes, manned by Commander Samson, with Lt Wedgwood Benn as observer, carried out photo reconnaissance, before dropping a 112 pound bomb on a gun position. Enemy fire damaged the aircraft and one bullet removed the heel from one of Cmdr Samson's shoes. He managed to land the aircraft on the water safely before the engine seized (this was not remarked on in the pages of the log). Samson was the Captain of the *Ben-my-Chree* and, as mentioned in Chapter Two, was one of the early pioneers of naval aviation. It is, to today's eyes, at the least unusual that the Captain would himself fly on an attack, given the risks. He would seem to have had the unshakeable confidence of the professional naval officer in his invulnerability. The effect on the Turkish defenders, who, despite firing on the aircraft would have experienced little or no aerial attack before, must have been enormous. The effect on the Arab residents of Jeddah would have been even greater. The likelihood that any would have seen aircraft before was slight; to see craft leaving the water and then drop bombs and machine gun Turkish positions from the air would have been beyond their comprehension. The aerial attack took less than an hour. That, combined with the bombardment from the five ships, caused a white flag to be raised over Jeddah shortly after the aerial attack. During the early morning of the next day, at 0300, a messenger from the Emir of Harb arrived on board *Fox* with a message for Boyle confirming that the Turkish garrison had surrendered. This comprised 45 officers, 1460 men and 16 guns. A large amount of military stores was also captured, which was of great use to the Arabs. Boyle signalled to *Ben-my-Chree* after the surrender that "probably the seaplanes decided the matter."[3] So, having decided the matter, *Ben-my-Chree* proceeded across the Red Sea to Port Sudan to take on coal.

Capturing Jeddah was a great success for the start of the revolt. A port of strategic importance, it gave access for supplies to be sent inland and gave an unrestricted means of communication with Cairo. The telegraph cable to Jeddah was quickly repaired; the navigation marks to aid ships entering the port were replaced so that it could be fully utilised. This allowed Egyptian artillery to be sent over from Port Sudan which then proceeded to Mecca to attack the Turkish barracks.

On 21 June *Dufferin* sailed from Jeddah to Port Sudan, arriving the next morning. She spent the next two days loading wheat and then, on the next day, embarked fifty troops, together with Lt Colonel C.C. Wilson and his staff, and returned to Jeddah, arriving the next morning, the 25th.

Lieutenant-Colonel Wilson, who was Governor of the Sudan Red Sea Province and also a Major General in the Egyptian Army, was installed as the British representative. He was given the official title of Pilgrimage Officer, so as not to upset Arab susceptibilities and fears, as Sherif Ali had shown with his attitude to naval observers landing during the attack on Jeddah. Wilson's presence had a major influence:

> "To the ability, tact and energy of this officer, whose obvious single mindedness and integrity completely won over the Arabs, the ultimate success of the rising is principally due."[4]

---

3. www.oca.269squadron.btinternet.co.uk "Squadron History 1914–1919".
4. *Naval Operations in the Red Sea 1916–1917*, 1925, 655.

This quote from the Naval Review was written in 1920, two years after the end of the war, when a clearer view than an immediate response was possible, although it was not published for a further five years. Meeting him in October, when he arrived in Jeddah, Lawrence did not share this opinion of Wilson, considering that his judgement was poor and that the information he was sending to Cairo was unreliable.[5] Wilson was equally unimpressed by Lawrence, very junior and an amateur to boot:

> "Lawrence wants kicking and kicking hard at that, and then he would improve ... He put every single person's back up I've met from the Admiral down."[6]

Lawrence's view of Wilson twelve months on had changed significantly. After the taking of Aqaba in July 1917 Lawrence returned to Jeddah aboard *Dufferin,*

> "where things became easy for me with Wilson's powerful help. He agreed that Aqaba was a most promising sector and to make it strong as soon as possible sent up a shipload of his reserve stores and ammunition and offered us any of his officers on loan. It was pleasant to find these two people, Wilson and Wingate [Governor-General of the Sudan], still preserving to the fourth year of the war the spirit which adopted as a matter of course the expedient promising best for the public interest. Especially he helped me with the King who came down from Mecca and talked discursively to us. Wilson had a wonderful influence in his councils because the Arabs always trusted him, sure of his single eye to their best interests. He was the King's touchstone by which to try doubtful courses. Thanks to him the proposed transfer of Faisal to Allenby's command was accepted at once ..."[7]

---

5. *Setting the Desert on Fire,* 60.
6. Wilson to Clayton, quoted in *Setting the Desert on Fire,* 60.
7. *Seven Pillars of Wisdom,* 352.

Fox had sailed from Jeddah on 18 June, leaving *Hardinge* and *Dufferin* who kept supplies and stores flowing into the port for the next month. *Fox* sailed down to Aden and later in the month was patrolling in the Southern Red Sea.

To the south of the Hejaz, the Asir region runs south towards Aden and is the home of the Idrissi tribe. The people of the northern portion of that region were loyal to Sherif Hussein, however those in the central and southern part gave their allegiance to Seyyid Mohammed who was known as the Idrissi and was supported, unofficially, by the Turks. The main port of the southern part of the Asir is Qunfunda[8] which lies about 200 miles south of Jeddah.

> "[It] is a small walled town with a Turkish garrison; on its southern side, without the walls, is a mosque and minaret … [It] has a small bazaar with supplies sufficient for the place only; but by giving notice and waiting a few days, a vessel may obtain cattle and sheep, as well as vegetables, from the interior (1881)."[9]

In order to try to enlist the Idrissi to the Sherifian cause, he was promised control of Qunfunda after the Turks had been removed. Accordingly *Fox,* accompanied by *Enterprise,* arrived off the port on 7 July, anchoring in the afternoon and joining *Suva* and *Minto* which had already arrived. Boyle invited the Turkish commander and a major of the Arab troops on board *Fox*, under a flag of truce, to dinner. As Boyle relates:

> "I gave them a good dinner and plenty of liquid including champagne, which was much appreciated by the Turk who amused himself during dinner by laughing at the Arab who was not quite

---

8. Also spelt Qunfida, Kunfunda or Kunfida, depending on the translator.
9. *Red Sea and Gulf of Aden Pilot*, 343. As this was unchanged in the 1909 edition, it would appear that there had been little change in the ensuing 28 years.

at home with his knife and fork. After dinner the time seemed opportune to suggest to the Turk that he should surrender. This I was anxious to get him to do, as I had not a large enough landing force to turn him out, and capture the garrison. He refused, but so half-heartedly that I did not anticipate much trouble and gave him until 9am to think it over."[10]

No reply was received the next morning by 0900 so, at 1000, the flag of truce came down and twenty minutes later the three ships opened fire, *Fox* targeting government offices, the Custom House and the officers' quarters, and *Suva* and *Minto* firing on Turkish trenches to the north and south of the town. After fifteen minutes of shelling, which was replied to by Turkish field guns, a white flag was raised over the town and the ships ceased fire. At 1330 a Turkish officer boarded *Fox* under a flag of truce and two hours later Boyle went ashore, with a guard of Marines, to receive the surrender. Ten officers, 195 men and two guns were captured. Boyle handed over the town to the two representatives of the Idrissi who were with him and then stayed ashore to witness the departure of the garrison which was shipped off to Egypt aboard *Suva* as prisoners of war within two hours. At their request, two officers and thirty sailors from *Fox* were left behind to protect the town from Bedouin attack until the arrival of the Idrissi Arabs three days later. (This shows a considerable lack of cohesion between the Arabs themselves.) During their stay as guards they had been sniped at, but there had been no concerted attack on them. On the arrival of the Arabs, *Minto* then returned *Fox*'s shore party to her.

Despite the removal of the Turkish garrison on 9 July, Qunfunda was not subdued. On 26 July *Suva* arrived and anchored there, where *Lunka* was already at anchor, and had been the guardship. On the evening of *Suva*'s arrival, just before midnight, for ten minutes, *Lunka*'s searchlight was switched on, lighting up the town, and she fired one warning round

---

10. *My Naval Life*, 98.

of gunfire. *Lunka* sailed the next morning and *Suva* moved into the inner anchorage. Twice that evening she shone her searchlight over the town to advertise her presence. She stayed there until 14 August, using her searchlight and firing her guns at night, using her steam cutter, mounted with a Maxim heavy machine gun and her other boats to help maintain order, as well as mounting shore patrols and having regular meetings with the Sheikh of the Idrissi in command of the town. Normally the Sheikh visited the *Suva*, but on one occasion the captain of *Suva*, Commander Henry Ritchie VC, went ashore for an evening meeting, accompanied by an armed boats crew. *Lunka* returned on 3 August with stores and mail for *Suva*. On 15 July *Minto* arrived to relieve *Suva*, who sailed for Port Sudan for repairs to her underwater engine intakes.

Returning to events at Jeddah after *Fox* left on 18 June, *Dufferin* had sailed three days later, crossing the Red Sea to Port Sudan, where she loaded a full cargo of bagged grain, her crew working long hours on the derricks swinging the cargo nets of grain into holds in the full heat of summer. Colonel Wilson and his staff boarded during the afternoon of the 24th, when she sailed for Jeddah two hours later, arriving there the next morning. After discharging her cargo into dhows, which lay alongside to take the cargo ashore, she sailed back to Port Sudan, taking with her fifty-one soldiers from the Warwickshire Regiment. Once again she loaded cargo for Jeddah, this time a cargo of flour. By the time this had been discharged it was the middle of July and she made her way to Suez, calling at Hassani Island, Yenbo (where she supported *Hardinge* in her attack – see below) and Aqaba en route. After taking on coal and loading stores she returned to Jeddah, discharging her cargo once again into dhows. She was there on the last day of the month, when she "dressed ship"[11] to mark the festival of Ramadan.

In August her role changed to that of personnel transport as, after embarking a guard from the Northamptonshire Regiment, she

---

11. "dressing ship" involves the complete display of flags from bow to stern, between the masts.

embarked 850 Turkish prisoners of war for passage to Suez. Losing no time she was back in Suez forty-eight hours later where the prisoners were disembarked, which took just two hours. Her log notes that some crockery and cutlery were broken or lost by one Turkish officer. There is no further explanation of this so one can only conjecture as to the events that may have caused the breakages. She returned to Jeddah and embarked a further 435 prisoners of war together with 123 Turkish women and children who had also been captured. On the day that she arrived back in Suez yet another Turkish officer was noted as having broken crockery. She anchored out in Suez Bay, discharged the prisoners and sailed again less than six hours later for Yenbo. Exactly a month after its capture, *Dufferin* returned there, this time to embark the Commander-in- Chief of the Arab forces at Medina for passage to Jeddah, where she arrived on the 29th. She sailed on the last day of the month, across the Red Sea to Port Sudan.

Hardinge was equally busy; arriving at Port Sudan on 19 June, she also loaded a full cargo for Jeddah; starting loading at 0930, she completed her cargo before 0500 the next morning, sailed less than thirty minutes later and arrived at Jeddah the same afternoon. Over the next four days her crew worked flat out unloading the cargoes into dhows, on one day loading thirty dhows over a ten-hour period. As July began she embarked passengers for Suez, including Ruhi, who was Storrs' agent and interpreter, Captain Cornwallis, of the Arab Bureau in Cairo and two other Arab officials. After landing her passengers there, and taking on coal, she loaded a cargo of rifles, ammunition, hand grenades and grain, this time with the assistance of the shore labour. Back at Jeddah on the 15th, finding *Dufferin* there, she commenced discharging her cargo into dhows with the aid, as in Suez, of shore labour.[12] *Suva* arrived on the 19th and transferred eight boxes of "specie" (gold coin). These

---

12. Her log for 17 July notes: "89 coolies from shore to work cargo until 1730." The reference to "coolies" implies the use of imported, possibly Chinese, labour, given the terms used at that time.

boxes, together with five more already on *Hardinge*, were discharged, under guard, for Grand Sherif Hussein. On the 27th both she and *Dufferin* were at Yenbo where they bombarded the Turkish fort, which hoisted a white flag after thirty minutes of firing by both ships. An Arab force was subsequently landed to take possession of the town. Having successfully taken Yenbo, *Hardinge* then sailed up the Gulf of Aqaba and spent the last two days of July at Aqaba, in company with *Raven*, the seaplane carrier. Using the latter's seaplanes for scouting purposes she fired on Turkish positions with her 4.7-inch guns.

By 3 August *Hardinge* was back at Suez where she spent two days coaling. She sailed for Jeddah on the 8th having received fifteen cases, as her log coyly remarks "said to contain specie" (i.e. gold), together with ammunition. She stopped off at Yenbo for two hours and arrived back at Jeddah on the 11th, finding *Fox* there and sending her provisions; this was yet another task of the RIM ships, acting as stores ships to the warships. Supplies had also been arriving on merchant ships; before *Hardinge*'s arrival, SS *Dakalieh*,[13] SS *Nairing* and HMT *Laomedon*[14] had been at Jeddah earlier in the month. She discharged her ammunition ashore, transferred thirteen of the fifteen cases "said to contain specie" to *Fox*, and embarked 768 prisoners of war together with a Petty Officer and eight ratings from *Fox* as guards, and sailed back to Suez within forty-eight hours, stopping briefly to bury a prisoner of war at sea.[15] She arrived in Suez on the 15th, took on coal, disembarked all the prisoners of war except one, who was ill, and sailed back to Jeddah on the same day. The prisoner of war who had been retained on board due to ill-health died the following day and was buried at sea. On her return to Jeddah, where she anchored the next day, she stayed there for a week. It must have been a welcome break for

13. Of the Khedivial Mail Line.
14. HMT (Hired Merchant Transport) *Laomedon* was hired from the Alfred Holt & Co subsidiary China Mutual Steam Ship Company. Of a similar size to *Northbrook* and *Hardinge*, in addition to cargo, she had accommodation for 200.
15 "One POW died 0445. Buried 0825." Little time was wasted.

her crew who had been working with little respite since the attack on Jeddah at the beginning of June. Boyle transferred to *Hardinge* the day after her arrival from *Fox*, who with *Suva* sailed for Suez. On the day of her departure, *Hardinge* loaded 600 Arab troops, eleven horses and two guns. Colonel Wilson and his staff embarked and she sailed for Yenbo, arriving the next morning. The Arab troops, horses and guns unloaded, she sailed for Suez later that day arriving on the 27th where Boyle and Wilson disembarked.

At the start of September, *Dufferin* had arrived in Port Sudan, sailing later on the 1st for Jeddah. She then went on to Ras Malak, where she met *Fox* before arriving at Yenbo, where a sheikh and twenty-four of his followers joined the ship for the passage to Suez. On arriving there she loaded 1,698 cases of rifles and ammunition, 12 mountain guns, and 7,979 packages of provisions, together with Colonel Wilson and his staff who boarded for her return to Yenbo, where she arrived on the 21st. She discharged part of her cargo of ammunition and provisions, loaded a seaplane and two field guns, embarked the Commander in Chief of Arab troops at Medina and two officers for the seaplane, and sailed less than eight hours later for Sherm Rabegh. Arriving there at 0900 the following morning, she spent the next week discharging stores, transferring the seaplane and its officers to the seaplane carrier *Anne*, and on the 28th sent her boats away with Arab troops to nearby Muttra.

Earlier in the month *Anne* had gone aground on the southern reef at Sherm Yenbo, where she was found by *Fox*. She had sent both an anchor and 3½ inch wire rope and then had sent a hawser across to help heave her off. This proved insufficient as the hawser parted; a heavy 5½ inch wire rope was then sent across.[16] Eventually *Anne* came off the reef ten hours after *Fox* had found her.

---

16. The author, having handled steel wire rope of this size, can attest that that this is much easier written than done.

The presence of *Dufferin, Fox* and *Espiegle* at Rabegh[17] in September was the result of the decision to use the harbour for the operation against Medina, which was too far north from Jeddah for it to be used.

"After slight trouble with the local Sheik, who proved to be pro-Turk, Arabs with Egyptian artillery and infantry landed there and by degrees a large base was established. The Egyptians constructed and entrenched camp and made roads while the Navy surveyed the harbour and built a timber pier which allowed of landing guns, motorcars, aeroplanes and large quantities of stores. *Minerva* (sic) [she was in Singapore at the time; the *Dufferin* was at Rabegh] was principally responsible for this work."[18]

Vice Admiral Wemyss, the Commander-in-Chief, noted in his report:

"On Thursday 28th September I proceeded round to Rabegh [from Jeddah] in HMS *Hardinge*. I had previously told the Captain of *Dufferin*, who was already there, to inform Ali Bey, the Grand Sherif's son, who commands the Arab forces at Rabegh of my intended visit; and that I hoped he would provide me and my staff with horses in order that I might myself inspect his positions and see how best I could help him with Naval guns. On my arrival the Captain of the *Dufferin* informed me that ever since his arrival there some few days before, Ali Bey had consistently thrown difficulties in the way of his landing, always postponing for 24 hours his proposed visit on some trivial excuse. I was not therefore very surprised when I received a message from Ali Bey to say that … he regretted it was impossible to take me around on that day. It seemed to me that this attitude on his part might arise

---

17. *The Red Sea and Gulf of Aden Pilot* said of Rabegh, "at the time of the survey in 1834, wood, water and other supplies were obtained at a cheap rate but the Bedouin Arabs were not to be implicitly trusted". Eighty-six years later many of the Naval officers still had a similar opinion of Bedouin Arabs.
18. *Naval Operations in the Red Sea 1916–17*, 656.

from any of the following circumstances. Firstly: either that he was afraid that as Christians our presence in the Hejaz might be resented by his followers; secondly: that he might be disinclined to let me see the poverty of his arrangements; or thirdly: that it might be intrigue on the part of some of his doubtful followers who look with cold eye on British assistance."[19]

The campaign to take Medina, which had a garrison of approximately 10,000 riflemen under Fakri Pasha, was a major undertaking. In addition to the works mentioned above,

> "Everything for the creation and maintenance both of this force, and the Arabs generally, had to be supplied from Egypt or the Sudan, and the ships of the patrol were kept busy transporting water, provisions, guns, munitions, uniforms, saddlery etc, as well as forage for both horses and camels. For this work the RIM ships[20] proved invaluable ... More Egyptian troops came across and proved exceedingly useful doing all the manual work required. The Arabs were content to look on, they would not work and although in considerable fear of a Turkish offensive could not be induced to dig for their own defence."[21]

It was at this point that Fakri Pasha, the energetic and active commander at Medina, was planning an attack on Mecca. The route from Medina to Mecca passes through Rabegh and, had he been able to recapture it, the revolt would have collapsed. Sherif Ali, with his younger half-brother Zeid was in command of Arab forces but had made no plans to defend the town. The perceived consequences of the fall of Rabegh were considered to be sufficiently grave that the dispatch of a brigade

---

19. Lord Wemyss Archive.
20. *Dufferin, Hardinge, Northbrook, Lama* and *Lunka*.
21. *Naval Operations in the Red Sea 1915–1917*, 656.

of British troops was entertained. The idea was eventually rejected, but three Royal Flying Corps planes did arrive and they, together with the Egyptian troops ashore and the presence of naval ships in the harbour, proved to be an adequate deterrent.

At Yenbo, which had been taken earlier, Sherif Feisal took over command. This port had a distillation plant for fresh water, which had been set up to provide for the pilgrims who passed through the port on their way to Mecca. This had been rendered unserviceable but was repaired by the Royal Navy and was, from then on, able to supply fresh water for all shore requirements. HMS *M31*, a monitor,[22] was sent down from Suez to be stationed as guard ship and the port was supplied by other transport ships to help reduce the load on the Red Sea Patrol ships.

In the middle of the month *Hardinge*, which had been at Yenbo, sailed to Wejh, where she transhipped the Arab troops that were on board to *Fox* and then sailed for Suez. She was to take a central role in a very different duty. Every year Cairo presented to Mecca a Holy Carpet (the Mahmal). This was not in reality a carpet but a Kiswa, which is a black brocade hanging with a border embroidered in gold with inscriptions from the Koran. This forms part of the decorations of the Keba, the pre-Islamic temple at Mecca, which houses the "Black Stone", the worship of which is the first duty of a pilgrim arriving at Mecca.[23] The holy carpet was accompanied by an escort of about 400 Egyptian troops and a sacred white camel. For the occasion the Egyptian troops wore the pilgrim costume required to accompany the Holy Carpet. They were commanded by an Egyptian Brigadier-General. Admiral Wemyss described the arrival of this officer on board *Euryalus*:

---

22. Monitors were small, shallow draft, heavily armed ships. M31 had two 6-inch guns but was only of 580 tons. She had a top speed of only 10 knots but her primary function was to provide an inshore gun platform for shore bombardment.
23. *My Naval Life*, 101.

"… When he arrived on board in his Pilgrim's costume consisting only of a somewhat scanty bath-sheet loosely wrapped round his person and kept together by a 'Sam-Browne' belt, I noticed that the guard of honour drawn up to receive him had some difficulty in keeping their countenances. On my returning his visit the situation was reversed. Myself in uniform, I was confronted by a guard and the band habited in Pilgrim attire, and it was I who now had difficulty keeping my countenance whilst the bandmaster was struggling to prevent his unaccustomed draperies from interfering with his duties of conducting."[24]

The preparations on the *Hardinge* for this task started the week before, shortly after her arrival at Suez, with the construction of stalls for the cavalry section of the escort. This was followed by loading ammunition and stores until, on 23 September, the embarkation of troops started. During the afternoon, according to her log, she "dressed ship rainbow fashion". A special train arrived from Cairo with the Holy Casket containing the Mahmal, which was embarked, together with sixteen cases "said to contain specie". Six hundred and fifty troops also boarded. The next day the ship prepared to sail. Fifty-seven horses, twenty-six mules and three camels were embarked together with more Arab soldiers. At 1730 she fired a twenty-one gun salute and sailed for Jeddah. *Euryalus*, with Admiral Wemyss and Ronald Storrs on board, had sailed just before *Hardinge*. *Fox* and *Perth* had also sailed to Jeddah, for saluting purposes and to provide a more impressive sight. *Espiegle* had transported Colonel Wilson and his staff. When *Hardinge* arrived on the 26th, she fired another twenty-one gun salute and again dressed ship "rainbow fashion". The next day Admiral Wemyss boarded and inspected the Egyptian guard. On the 28th *Hardinge* once again dressed ship rainbow fashion at 0600, and Admiral Wemyss and his staff, together with Boyle, from *Fox*, boarded to observe the

---

24. *Lord Wester Wemyss*, 330.

Mahmal leave the ship, accompanied by a nineteen gun salute. Three hours after that she sailed for Rabegh, taking Storrs to join *Espiegle* there, returning straight away to Jeddah.

Ronald Storrs, who had accompanied Admiral Wemyss, kept a diary of the trip, and relevant extracts give a different description of the occasion:

"26.ix.16 Passed through the dangerous but well buoyed Jeddah Reef about 3.30 to find *Hardinge* dressed and flying Egyptian flag at peak with green three crescented ensign at head to note she was carrying the Mahmal, which indeed was plainly visible on deck ... Cannot help wishing that our speed might have exceeded $8^1/_3$ knots (which I now find it to have been) so that we might have had more time here. Weather very hot, damp, windless and oppressive ...

27.ix.16 Leaving *Euryalus* at 9:30 AM, we steamed towards the town of Jeddah, and drew up at a little jetty to a salute of eighteen guns fired from antique mortars. We were received by the local notables and by Wilson ... After lunch ... I walked down through the town past the Municipality to the jetty in order to meet, and take on board *Euryalus,* Sherif Mohsin and his friends [which they reached about 4 PM.] ... The Sherif and his party were shown over the more easily understood features of *Euryalus.* The big guns so astonished them that they could not at first believe them to be guns at all ... As an immediate and tangible result of the afternoon's proceedings, the Admiral was officially invited to ride at the head of the procession through Jeddah of the Holy Carpet itself, which we prudently, if reluctantly, thought fit to decline.

28.ix.16 Rose 5.30 and left ship with Admiral and staff at 6.30, reaching town just after seven, there to find for about the fifth time the hour for the Mahmal procession had been changed and that it would not start till 9. The Admiral, whose life has been passed in the cultivation of exactitude, abandoned himself upon this to a mournful indignation: mingled with a wrathful surprise at my lack of astonishment. We decided to watch the landing from the roof of the Quarantine Office ... Back directly to *Hardinge*, *bateau de luxe* which, as more than one sense reminded one, had conveyed the Mahmal, horses, camels *and* pilgrims from Suez to Jeddah."[25]

Admiral Wemyss had arranged for Storrs to be returned to Suez, so he joined *Espiegle* in Rabegh, where *Hardinge* had taken him. *Espiegle* was a small, elderly naval sloop which was still rigged with masts and yards for sail, although no sails were carried. Although her stated top speed was 13½ knots, her actual top speed by 1916 was no more than 8 knots. She sailed for Suez on 29 September. Storrs did not enjoy the trip:

"Three days all but six hours in *Espiegle* should serve as a warning against the excessive zeal of such as hasten back to their work. *Espiegle* is far smaller than the classic Channel boats, and without any of even their few amenities. The commander [by then Commander R. Fitzmaurice had replaced Commander Betts] thrice informed me that the ship's bottom was 2 inches deep in barnacles, that the engines could never remotely approach their indicated maximum of 13½ knots, that the tide at once took off one knot, that in the Gulf of Suez it was all he could do to keep her under way – finally that he was very short of coal. If we "got it stiff" in the Gulf we should be lucky in arriving at Suez on Monday at all. After a less than frugal lunch (no ice aboard) made an attempt to read ... But gave it up and laid, practically for the rest of the voyage, a high-heaved and higher-heaving log of uncomplaining misery. The natural filth of the vessel, which was great, was constantly increased by the dense pitiless descent

---

25. *Orientations*, 169.

of greasy black smuts vomited up by the bad coal. At every (perpetual) larger wave the ship struck her nose into it with a hammer-like blow, while of course the screw and the engine raced in jangling discord."[26]

In the nearly four month period from June, when this chapter began, ships of the Red Sea Patrol had taken Jeddah, Qunfunda, Yenbo, Wejh and Rabegh, taking over 1,700 Turkish prisoners of war from the various ports to prisoner of war camps in Egypt. They had supplied Jeddah continuously, carried troops from the Sudan, protected Qunfunda, provided a guardship at Yenbo and provided transport for the Holy Carpet. They had built a port at Rabegh, restored the navigation buoys for the entrance to Jeddah, and rebuilt the water distillation plant at Yenbo. The seaplanes had carried out reconnaissance and bombing missions. At the time this almost complete dependence on the Royal Navy was an official secret, as the Allied propaganda organisation needed the world to know that the Arab Revolt was no more than that – an Arab revolt. Lawrence James notes:

"The summer campaign in Hejaz set the pattern for the future. Arab irregulars could never hope to engage, let alone overcome Turkish troops in open battle without substantial assistance. Until the end of the war the Arabs would depend on endless transfusions of Allied arms and ammunition as well as British gold to keep their forces in the field ... Their bases at Jeddah, Rabegh, Yanbu al Bahr [Yenbo], and later al Wajh [Wejh] and Aqaba would be protected by British and French men-of-war."[27]

The lion's share of that protection was undertaken by the ships of the Red Sea Patrol.

---

26. Ibid. 170.
27. *The Golden Warrior*, 162.

Russian Cruiser *Aurora*, with casemate guns on side (St Petersburg, 2013). *(Author's collection)*

Casemate guns, Aurora. *(Author's collection)*

Mukalla, Aden Protectorate (Admiralty Pilot 1909).

Admiralty steam cutter. From the flag in the forepart, photographed supporting diving operations. *(R. Partis, by permission)*

Arab craft off Jedda,
October 1916.
(Author's collection)

The Holy Carpet
arriving in Jedda,
October 1916.
(Author's collection)

Egyptian Brigadier in "escort rig" (sheet & Sam Browne belt), escorting the Holy Carpet, October 1916. *(Author's collection)*

Holy Carpet coming ashore in Jedda, October 1916. *(Author's collection)*

Aqaba from the sea, 1917.

Arabian Dhow.

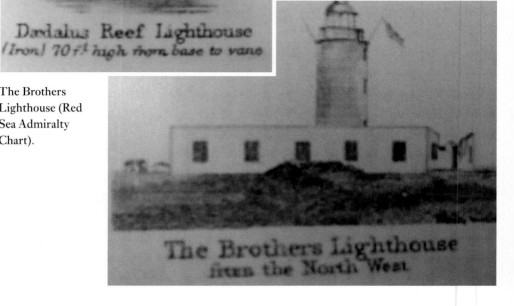

Daedalus Reef Light house (Red Sea Admiralty Chart).

Daedalus Reef Lighthouse
(Iron) 70 ft high from base to vane

The Brothers Lighthouse (Red Sea Admiralty Chart).

The Brothers Lighthouse
from the North West

George Carew's dress medals, Legion d'Honneur (l) Distinguished Service Cross (r). *(Captain J. Carew, by permission)*

George Carew, Lieutenant RNR, DSC, Legion d'Honneur. *(Captain J. Carew, by permission)*

Jeddah 1917.

TE Lawrence.

Suez Canal at Tussum. The high
bank of the Canal here obstructed
Hardinge's gun aimers – see p.40.
(Author's collection)

see p.40.

The Holy Carpet being
paraded through Cairo,
1916.

Captain W. Boyle, as Admiral of the Fleet the Earl of Cork and Orrery. *(Earl of Cork & Orrery, by permission)*

Meeting on board *Dufferin*, at which the date and time of the Arab Revolt was decided. (Back row, second left R.Storrs, end right Commander Warren(Captain, *Dufferin*). Front Row first left Sherif Zeid, end right captain Boyle). *(Earl of Cork and Orrery, by permission)*

The Holy Carpet being taken ashore, on two cutters, at Jeddah in 1917. *(Earl of Cork and Orrery, by permission)*

Sherifs Feisal (fourth left) and Zeid (second left) on board *Suva*, Yenbo 1917. *(Earl of Cork and Orrery, by permission)*

The Royal Navy constructing a jetty at Rabegh. *(Imperial War Museum)*

On the deck of *Dufferin*, Wej, 1917. *(Imperial War Museum)*

Chapter Six

"My Super-Cerebral Friend": October 1916–January 1917

HMS Minerva

Built in 1895, by 1914 her top speed could only be maintained for short periods.

On the 12 October, Storrs took the train from Cairo to Suez, to board *Lama* for the passage to Jeddah. He had with him "little Lawrence, my super-cerebral friend".[1] Lawrence describes Storrs' conduct on the *Lama*:

---

1. *Orientations*, 171.

"Storrs was an intolerant brain and seldom stooped to his company. On this occasion he was more abrupt even than ever. He turned twice round the deck, sniffed 'no-one worth talking to', and at once sat down in one of the two comfortable armchairs and began a deep discussion of Debussy with Aziz el Masri, in the other … The ship's officers found it an unnecessary conversation, but could not interrupt it."

Lawrence goes on to describe his conversation with the captain of the *Lama*, Captain Scott, who was a naval hydrographer:

"[He] led me off to cooler places, and we found common interests in revolver shooting and marine survey and a common antipathy in coral reefs. The eastern coast of the Red Sea was fringed with reefs, mostly uncharted, and on them the patrol vessels were constantly going ashore. It did no harm, indeed, it did good, for the clean, gritty coral-fringes used to scrape from the ships bottoms the accumulated weed of the past few months; but seamen were prejudiced against going aground and these Red Sea captains could not overcome their training. Scott had been a famous victim on one occasion. He had spent weeks down near Kameran charting a dangerous area on the map, and was on his way home, triumphantly navigating on his new-drawn sheet, when he piled up the ship on a reef omitted from his work, because it, and it only, was adequately entered on the old chart. However, no one could throw stones at him, for every ship in the fleet had been ashore, except the *Hardinge* which claimed a clean slate but had to admit to broken rudders!"[2]

Lama arrived in Jeddah on the 16th, after what, in Lawrence's words, was "the usual pleasant run to Jidda, in the delightful sea-climate of

2. *Seven Pillars of Wisdom*, 47

the Red Sea, never too hot while the ship was moving."[3] On arrival, Colonel Wilson sent his launch out to *Lama*, to carry Lawrence and Storrs ashore.

Dufferin (Commander Warren) was still supplying Jeddah; she was in Suez on the 23rd, having arrived with yet another batch of Turkish prisoners of war from there, then loading 7,008 sacks of flour, 396 tins of coffee, 812 bales of hay and 1,000 boxes of ammunition, which she delivered to Jeddah three days later, sailing after discharging her cargo, twenty-four hours later, for Port Sudan. There a contingent of 165 troops of the Egyptian Army boarded for passage to Rabegh.

At the beginning of November, *Suva*, with Boyle now in command (*Fox* had gone to Bombay for a refit in dry dock), arrived at Yenbo, whence Lawrence had gone from Jeddah. His first meeting with Boyle has already been described but, nevertheless, Boyle agreed that Lawrence could take passage in *Suva* to Jeddah, where *Euryalus* was in port, with Vice Admiral Wemyss on board. Lawrence persuaded Wemyss to take him to Port Sudan. *Euryalus* sailed on the 4th November, for the short hop across the Red Sea. (Lawrence's presence on board was not noted in her log.) Lawrence noted of Wemyss:

> "[He] had taken the greatest interest in the Arab revolt from the beginning ... He had given the Arabs guns and machine guns, and landing parties and technical help and unlimited transport, and naval co-operation, always making a pleasure of our requests and fulfilling them in overflowing measure. Had it not been for his goodwill, and the admirable way in which Captain Boyle gave effect to it, the jealousy of Sir Archibald Murray would have wrecked the rebellion at its start. As it was, Sir Rosslyn Wemyss acted Godfather till the Arabs were on their feet."[4]

---

3. Ibid.
4. *Seven Pillars of Wisdom*, 98.

Dufferin was still in Rabegh. After discharging her cargo, her crew were put to work strengthening the pier that had been built earlier in the year and then clearing and blasting out the channel to the landing place. Some of the cargo, of horses and stores, was transferred (or "cross-decked" to use the modern term) to *Hardinge*. *Suva* also arrived at Rabegh, bringing a contingent of troops, who arrived on the 11th. *Dufferin*'s crew assisted *Suva* in the discharge of her cargo. Four days later, *Dufferin* sailed from Jeddah, preparing her holds on the way for another load of Turkish prisoners of war; arriving in the early afternoon, she embarked the prisoners who were all on board by 1830. She sailed twelve hours later for Suez, where they were disembarked forty-eight hours later.

The absence of *Fox*, off on her refit, meant that the other ships had to work harder to cover her absence. So *Suva*, meanwhile, with Boyle, returned to Qunfunda where she stayed until the eighth; she then sailed to Port Sudan. Arriving two days later, she berthed alongside the quay, loading stores and troops for Rabegh. She spent the morning so doing, and with all troops embarked and all stores loaded, sailed at midday. She was back in Jeddah at eight o'clock the next morning, the 12th, closely followed by *Euryalus* and *Minerva*, which had returned from the Far East at the end of October. The latter sailed for Rabegh the next day, where she was stationed for the next month as guard ship. The *Minerva*'s space in Jeddah harbour was taken by *Hardinge* which had arrived from Yenbo and spent the next five days at anchor before sailing for Rabegh, where she loaded horses, ammunition and troops for Yenbo. She arrived and anchored there on the 22nd finding *Scotia* and *Lama* there also at anchor.

Suva stayed in Jeddah until the 15th and then she, too, steamed up to Rabegh, where she landed stores then moved across the harbour, to allow *Minerva* to take her place so as to carry out her duties as guard ship. Later that day she sailed to Yenbo to discharge cargo and specie. From there she sailed to Suez, arriving on 22 November, where she stayed until the end of the month, to allow her officers and crew some days of shore leave, after a prolonged period of action.

Despite the best efforts of the ships of the Red Sea Patrol carrying stores, ammunition and gold to supply the Arab Revolt, the regular troops of the Turkish army were more than a match for the Arabs. In order to bolster the Arab tribesmen, a trained force, recruited from the people of Mecca and Ta'if, together with some Turkish prisoners of war of Arab extraction who changed their allegiance, was put under the command of Sherif Ali. All the supplies and equipment for this force were part of the stores that came down from Suez. By October the force was considered to be sufficiently trained to go into action against the Turks. They went into action against the outposts at Medina but were driven back by the Turks to Rabegh. Only the presence of *Dufferin*, *Lama* and *Anne* in the port, the guns and seaplanes of which provided enough of a threat to stop the advancing enemy from attacking, prevented the Turks from re-taking Rabegh.

Sir Reginald Wingate, the Governor-General of the Sudan, wrote to Vice Admiral Wemyss at the end of November:

"I am very grateful for all you are doing to help matters in the Hedjaz. There, as elsewhere in the world, the splendid work of the Navy and their readiness to cooperate for the general good is one of the few wholly satisfactory features. What we should have done without your assistance and practical advice I really do not know. As regards the Arab' military situation at Rabegh particularly and in the Hedjaz generally, I sincerely hope the opinions expressed in your telegram to the Admiralty will prove correct. There is nevertheless the contingency that a reverse to Faisal or one of the other brothers or some unforeseen accident may cause a panic and cause the Turks to take the offensive. The situation in that case would, I believe, change with surprising and embarrassing rapidity and I do not want this contingency to be ignored by the War Office in view of the fact that so far as I can see, only by the arrival of regular troops could the situation and the morale of the Arabs be restored … I am opposing the latest proposal to move the main base and training ground from Rabegh. It is no good constantly changing plans, and unless we stick to our intention and carry it through we run grave risks of doing nothing (with the able cooperation of our Allies, Arab and others.) All sorts of subsidiary questions are cropping up – including … jurisdiction over foreigners in the Hejaz, where of course the Sharia is the sole legal system. I'm not going to be carried in these matters and I am anxious – particularly in regard to the latter (foreign jurisdiction) – not to have my hand forced. On this account and in view of the numbers of foreigners (British and others) with the Arabs, and not a little nervous of tactless handling of the latter by the former leading to an incident, I have had all my people warned that they must be most careful in their treatment of all Arabs (and Egyptians, particularly officers) and courtesy and patience are very necessary. I mention this as in view of the number of RNR and non-regular personnel in Boyle's command you might think it a wise precaution to issue a word of warning on the subject to all concerned. 'Prevention is better than cure' …"[5]

In early December, when *Suva* had returned from Suez, she was in Yenbo when Feisal and his men were forced to retreat there. Boyle, still in command, described the scene from the ship:

"… On deck early one morning I saw a blaze of colour on the shore horizon looking rather like the lower end of a rainbow moving towards the harbour. As it got nearer I saw what looked like trunks of tall trees underneath the colour, and it was not until some minutes later that with my glasses I made it out to be a large force of Arabs on camels moving in the shape of a 'V' towards the town. It was of course the legs of the camels that looked like the

---

5. Wemyss papers 4/3 (5).

Yenbo town from the anchorage.

Yenbo. *(Admiralty Pilot 1909)*

trunks of trees, the whole phenomena being due to mirage which is always greatest at sunrise & sundown. At the apex of the 'V' rode the two Sharifs and Lawrence,[6] and the phalanx was made up of Feisal's retainers and escort, all wearing robes of brilliant colours. The effect had a striking though not warlike appearance, but the actual fighting men were holding off the Turks who were pursuing the retreating Arabs down to the hills bordering the coastal plain, about 6 miles inland. Fortunately I had with me in the harbour the seaplane carrier *Anne* and a spirited attack made by her aircraft, together with the presence of three other ships prevented an attack on the town, defences of which were very rudimentary."[7]

The Arabs, under Feisal's command, and with the assistance of Lawrence, defended Yenbo to the best of their ability; they were aided by the fact that the town was elevated from the surrounding area on a coral reef, which rose about twenty feet above sea level and had the sea on two sides.

The five ships now in Yenbo included *M31*, the monitor, whose shallow draft and 6-inch guns made her ideal for coastal defence work. Her searchlights, together with those of *Dufferin* were able to light up

---

6. Lawrence was not with the two Sherifs: "I was called out again by the news that Sharif Zeid was coming, and went down to the walls to see the beaten force ride in." *Seven Pillars of Wisdom*, 117. Given the visibility, even with binoculars it would have been almost impossible to recognise an individual on a camel.

7. *My Naval Life*, 100.

the plain beyond the town, to prevent a night attack. There was one such attempt to mount a night offensive. The Turkish troops had been guided down "to rush Yenbo in the dark and stamp out Feisal's Army once and for all: but that their hearts had failed them at the silence, and the blaze of lighted ships end to end of the harbour and the slow beams of the searchlights revealing the openness of the glacis they would have to cross. So they turned back, and that night I believe, the Turks lost the war." It is very obvious that, without the presence of these five ships in the harbour, Lawrence could not have made that comment. He added:

> "Personally, I was on the *Suva*, to be undisturbed, and sleeping splendidly at last ... though we might have won a glorious victory I was ready to give much more for just that one night's unbroken rest."[8]

About eighty miles north of Yenbo, as the crow flies, is the harbour of Umm Lejh, on the shore close to Hassani Island, which was a regular anchorage for the ships of the Red Sea Patrol. In mid-December, a force of Arabs was moved there by ship. The Naval Review commented:

> "a force of several hundred Arabs was put on board the patrol vessels (and particularly unpleasant passengers they proved)."[9]

This was yet another move northwards, taking Umm Lejh and so pushing the Turkish forces further back, taking control of the coast all the way from Jeddah, nearly 250 miles to the south.

Hardinge arrived at Yenbo the day after *Suva* had sailed to Rabegh, to discharge her cargo of stores and mules. Sailing the same afternoon she arrived at Jeddah the next morning in time to dress

---

8. *Seven Pillars of Wisdom*, 121.
9. *Naval Review*, 658.

ship and fire a twenty-one gun salute to the mark the arrival of the Grand Sherif. He inspected a French cruiser, *Portheau*, and then inspected *Hardinge* and *Suva*, which fired yet another twenty-one gun salute. When *Hardinge* had completed her ceremonial duties, she discharged eight cases of specie later in the evening. The next morning she embarked a contingent of Arab troops for Rabegh and sailed southwards along the coast, arriving there at 1400. *Euryalus* arrived shortly afterwards, stopping off there for twenty-four hours en route from Suez to Aden. *Hardinge* took over *Minerva*'s place as guard ship until 22 December.

Suva sailed from Jeddah back to Yenbo, taking with her fourteen cases of military stores. She had sailed during the afternoon, but did not arrive at Yenbo until the following morning. Entering port in the hours of darkness with no shore lights to navigate by was not possible, so she steamed at reduced speed through the night. Dawn was at about 0530 and she entered Sherm Yenbo four hours later, making fast alongside *Dufferin* to take on fresh water. With her fresh water tanks replenished, she entered Yenbo harbour and anchored there. She was to stay there until the 22nd, and during that period some of her crew were ashore erecting a water tank and repairing the condensing plant for the supply of fresh water. Lawrence had sailed with Boyle from Yenbo to Rabegh on the 12th; *Suva*'s log noted that Lawrence left the ship on 22 December, so it is possible that he had stayed on board for ten days as *Suva* sailed on to Jeddah and back to Yenbo.

At this time in December, with the retreats by Feisal and Ali, it seemed that the Arab Revolt was very near collapse, due predominantly to the ineffective nature of the Arabs in battle and the incompetence of their leaders, despite Lawrence's comments at Yenbo ("that night … the Turks had lost the war"). However *Raven*, which was still at Yenbo, had continued flying offensive sorties with her seaplanes over the Turkish positions. On the 16th whilst flying a reconnaissance mission, they noted that there appeared to be a withdrawal by Turkish troops, which eased the pressure on Yenbo. The Red Sea Patrol and the Royal Naval Air Service, yet again, had had a significant effect on events ashore.

Midway through December Sherif Ali and his force had retreated to Rabegh pursued by Turkish forces. There was a strong possibility that the Turkish commander, Fakhri, could advance on Rabegh with very little to hinder him on the way. The situation was sufficiently serious for evacuation plans to be made. *Hardinge* was in port as guard ship until the 22nd when *Minerva* returned to take her place. *Suva* arrived on the 23rd from Yenbo with reinforcements, stores and ammunition. Anchoring at 0900, disembarkation of the troops and discharge of the stores started twenty minutes later and was completed in three hours. On the 24th a conference ashore decided that a defensive position by the airstrip, manned by the Egyptian Army and a party of *Minerva*'s crew, defended by *Minerva*'s guns and assisted by the Royal Flying Corps would act as a sufficient deterrent to the advancing Turks. On the same day as the conference *Suva* had sailed for Port Sudan arriving at nine o'clock on Christmas Day. Half an hour after arriving, Divisions, at which the whole ship's company was assembled on deck, was held and, the log records, "a message from HM the King was read to the ship's company by the Captain". The rest of the day the crew were allowed to relax. In the afternoon special leave was given to the starboard watch from 1400 to 2030. How much there was to enjoy in Port Sudan on Christmas Day 1916 it is hard to tell. Boxing Day was not a day of rest for *Suva* as coaling started at 0700 and carried on for the next seven hours. At the same time as coaling, sixty live sheep and three hundredweights of fodder were embarked. She then returned to Rabegh overnight, arriving the following morning. She transferred ten of her sheep to *Minerva*.[10] She stayed there for the next two days, during that time landing a three-pounder gun and eighty rounds of ammunition to augment the shore defences.

---

10. Her log does not record the discharge of any further sheep to shore or other ships, so it must be assumed that fifty sheep were kept on board for a supply of mutton for the crew.

From there she sailed to Aden, at her best speed of 9½ knots. She arrived there on 3 January and made fast to buoys in the harbour. Shore leave was granted and the ship's steam cutter ferried men ashore; the last boat returned at 2100. At 0200 the next morning the Second Engineer, Lieutenant Commander Rowe RNR, went into the Engineer Commander's cabin, as the log notes: "behaving in an improper manner" and swearing at him. It is possible that Rowe had been ashore to celebrate the New Year, three days late, and had returned drunk, or that there had been a party in one of the engineers' cabins. The next morning he was brought before Captain Boyle and "logged" – that is, the details of the offence were entered in the ship's log, and would also have been noted on his service record. Boyle and Rowe both signed the log, the latter to agree that he understood the offence that had been committed. However, not only was he disciplined for that offence, he was also logged for failing to control the three junior engineer officers, Lieutenant Jordan, and Sub Lieutenants Taylor and Criddle, when they collected at, in the log's words, "an improper time and place to express discontent with an order issued by the Engineer Commander". Taylor was also disciplined for having taken a leading part in the improper assembly. The engineer officers, all RNR, almost certainly would have been her peacetime Merchant Navy engineers. The conduct of Rowe, in entering the Engineer Commander's cabin to wake him up and abuse him would have been, and is still, unacceptable in a merchant ship: on a ship flying the White Ensign – and therefore a warship – in a time of war, is at a level well above unacceptable. For the Engineer Lieutenant and Sub Lieutenants to conspire against the Engineer Commander is even more serious and, in naval terms is close to mutiny. Later in the log it notes that on 31 January, the day *Suva* left Aden to sail to Bombay, Rowe and Jordan again treated the Engineer Commander with contempt.

The behaviour of the engineer officers, although exceedingly unusual, suggests some possible alternative reasons: the Engineer Commander, Lieutenant Commander Ferguson, RNR (who, most likely, would have been her Chief Engineer in peacetime) was not a popular officer and his conduct may have been such that the junior officers could not continue without making a protest. For the Second Engineer, Rowe, to have permitted this would have been either very unlikely, or indicative of a Chief Engineer who was a thoroughly unpleasant person, and had made life unbearable for those under his command. The other alternative was that the engineers, who, before the war, were the engineers on what had been a South Pacific banana boat, before being requisitioned for Naval purposes, were accustomed to standards of behaviour that were much lower than the Royal Navy would tolerate.

Reading between the lines of the report in the log, the night of 4 January would have been a lively one in the engineers' accommodation. An altercation in the Chief Engineer's cabin would not have gone unnoticed. The "improper assembly" referred to may have been a rowdy drunken party in another cabin, from which Rowe went to express his views, in a forceful manner, to the Engineer Commander. The further incident at Aden at the end of the month would have been enough to ensure that both Rowe and Jordan would have been unlikely to retain their RNR commissions beyond November 1918 – even had they wanted to, which was probably very unlikely. What in naval terms was close to mutiny was, to them, probably nothing more than a good New Year's party.[11]

In January, it was decided that a further step north was necessary. Wejh was a further eighty miles north. In order to take it, troops were to be taken from Yenbo. Lawrence received a letter as he reached there with Feisal, from Commander Warren of *Dufferin*, asking for details of the local situation before embarking Sherif Zeid and his troops.

---

11. In the 1960s, on board a BP tanker in port, the Chief Officer was asleep in his cabin when he was awoken by the sound of running water. On investigating, he found one of the cadets in his office, urinating on his office chair. This drunken episode was dealt with informally: "… after he had scrubbed out my cabin!"

Dufferin was anchored at Sherm Yenbo, a few miles north, so not in a position to keep up with the changing situation in the main port. Lawrence found this frustrating:

"… it was a point of old friction between us. Warren was well-meaning, but had not the breadth of Boyle, the fiery politician and constitutionalist, or the brain of Linberry of *Hardinge*, who filled himself with the shore gossip of any port he touched, and who took a personal interest in the life of all classes on his beat. Warren looked on the land as a thing sometimes tied up to, sometimes run into, and its inhabitants as people out to exploit the Navy."[12]

In the meantime, Boyle had given passage to Lawrence, on *Suva*, and had arrived at Umm Lejh on the 12th. Boyle had been there earlier, on *Fox*, and bombarded the Turkish garrison there, destroying their barracks. He and Lawrence went ashore and walked over to the fort which had been shelled by *Fox*. Lawrence noted:

"Boyle looked at the ruins and said, 'I'm rather ashamed of myself for smashing such a potty place.' He was a very professional officer."[13]

On the 16th Major Vickery, of the British Military mission arrived, and he, Lawrence, and Boyle went from there to visit Feisal. He, with his tribesmen, was camped about ten miles inland. This entailed a camel ride. Although Lawrence and Vickery were experienced camel riders, this was a skill not normally possessed by Royal Navy officers and Boyle was no exception:

---

12. *Seven Pillars of Wisdom*, 133. Warren was by no means alone in his view that the inhabitants of the land were people out to exploit the Navy.
13. *Seven Pillars of Wisdom*, 136

"Except as a child at the Zoo, or going to the Pyramids as a tourist, I had never mounted one, and I endured agonies pumping up and down, generally some distance astern trying to keep up."

He was further discomforted by the conditions in Feisal's camp and the meal that was offered:

"On arrival we found a great encampment of camel skin tents in the centre of which stood Feisal's. It was a striking scene, but the absence of any sanitary precautions made it an unpleasant place on a hot day. Feisal gave us luncheon, at which we sat on the ground and ate out of a large bowl which was stood on ammunition boxes in front of him. In it was a greasy stew out of which we helped ourselves to pieces of meat with our fingers. Faisal handed me choice morsels and I understood that this was a special mark in favour to his principal guest, so I felt obliged to eat them. Vickery saved the situation by producing a large flask of whisky, a proceeding frowned on by Lawrence, but laughed at by Feisal, and the contents were very welcome."[14]

As a result of the discussions and decisions made that day, *Hardinge* was to take 400 Arabs to Wejh. Boyle described *Hardinge* as a ship that was always in the forefront of the action and because of its size and construction, was particularly suited for this sort of work. He also agreed with Lawrence's view of Linberry, her captain, who in Boyle's view had gained a great reputation on the coast. It had been decided, by Feisal, advised in part by Lawrence, that Yenbo would be evacuated. All the Arabs from there, both regular Arab army and Feisal's tribesmen would be moved to Wejh. There was, in this decision, a risk that Turkish forces would re-occupy Yenbo. It followed, therefore, that as much of the stores and equipment as possible would be moved up

---

14. *My Naval Life*, 102.

the coast. In addition to the 400 Arabs, *Hardinge* was loaded with all the stores, rifles, ammunition, high explosive and petrol: over 1,000 tons in total. She was then to remain at Wejh – or as near as she could safely be, as it was a very small port and too small for *Hardinge* to enter – as a source of supplies, food and water.

Lawrence noted:

> "for the actual attack on Wejh we offered Boyle an Arab landing party of several hundred men, Harb and Juheina peasantry and slaves under Saleh ibn Shefia, Mohammad's young son. He was negroid, but a pleasant boy, of good courage, with the faculty of friendliness. He kept his men in reasonable order by conjurations and appeals and never minded how much his own dignity was outraged by them, or by us. Boyle accepted, and decided to put them on another deck of the all-embracing *Hardinge*, whose stomachs seemed as plentiful as a camel's. We agreed that they with the naval party should be landed to the north of the town, where the Turks had no post to block a landing, and from which flank Wejh village and harbour were best turned. Boyle would have at least six ships, carrying 50 guns to occupy the Turks minds; and a seaplane ship to direct the guns."[15]

On the 20th, the day before *Hardinge* embarked her cargo, *Suva* had moved out to Hassani Island, about nine miles off Umm Lejh. This was in order to meet *Fox*, which had returned from her refit, for Boyle to transfer back to her. *Suva* sailed later that day, under the command of her First Lieutenant.

Wejh had been the subject of an attack the previous autumn. It was known to be held at that time by a substantial Turkish contingent, supported by the local Billi tribe. *Hardinge*, *Fox* and *Anne* had met at Umm Lejh and sailed in line astern up the coast to Wejh. They arrived

---

15. *Seven Pillars of Wisdom*, 138.

on 13 September and opened fire just after sunrise, continuing until mid-morning. Despite this bombardment, and aerial attacks from *Anne*'s seaplanes, the Turkish defence held. Without troops to back up the bombardment there was no prospect of occupying the town, so the ships withdrew.

The next assault on Wejh was a combined assault with the Arabs from *Hardinge* attacking from the sea and the regular Arab army advancing on foot to attack from the land.

There is a difference in the reports of the troops carried to Wejh by *Hardinge*. In the Naval Review, she embarks 400 Arabs, which are disembarked approximately twenty miles south of Wejh. According to *Hardinge*'s log, they are disembarked at Sherm Habbam, a small inlet in the coast about ten miles south of Wejh. Jeremy Wilson, on the other hand, comments that: "550 Arabs judged to be of indifferent quality were to be put on *Hardinge* and landed on the far side (i.e. North) of the town."[16] (This equates with Lawrence's account in *Seven Pillars of Wisdom*). Yet another voice, that of Wemyss, states, "I have embarked some 2,000 Arabs."[17] As *Hardinge* was the only ship that loaded troops it would seem that Wemyss significantly overestimated the numbers on board.

Wemyss had sailed down from Suez on the Naval Yacht *North Star*, for meetings with the Red Sea Patrol and also ashore at Rabegh. He then arrived off Hassani Island, where *North Star* anchored. From there he went ashore:

"I have been at anchor off a desert island in the Red Sea for the last 24 hours, and this morning I landed and inspected a heterogeneous "army" with which on Tuesday we had to capture the Turkish town of Wej[h] and its garrison. My one fear is that the garrison will bolt before we can capture them. We are working

---

16. *Lawrence of Arabia*, 350.
17. *Life and Letters of Lord Wester Wemyss*, 346.

in conjunction with the Arabs, really an extraordinary affair. I have four ships here and some seaplanes, and I have embarked some 2000 Arabs. In the meantime an Arab force is approaching from the land side and on Tuesday morning we hope to have surrounded the place. By all the rules of the game the Turkish garrison should surrender. But if they don't I very much doubt the Arabs attacking them. However with the ships' guns and such seamen as I can land to stiffen them, I don't expect they will hold out ... I am in hopes that with this place in the hands of our Allies(!) the Arabs, the situation in the Hedjaz will be materially improved ... At this moment many dhows are depositing their freights of Arabs on board one of the ships [*Hardinge*] and a picturesque sight it is. But it is one of the extraordinary offshoots of the universal war that British men-of-war should be co-operating with Arab hordes!"[18]

There were in fact five ships, *Hardinge, Fox, Espiegle, Suva* and *Anne*, the latter with her seaplanes. They sailed up the coast and arrived at the rendezvous to meet Feisal's army who were on the march, but after twenty-four hours, there was no sign of them. The operation was then executed in their absence. *Hardinge* had anchored off Sherm Habbam, and the next morning moved in to land the Arabs, using both her boats and also *Espiegle*'s in addition, after which she moved along the coast and opened fire on Wejh, together with *Fox, Suva & Espiegle*. *Anne*'s seaplanes were attacking from the air. A party of seamen and marines from the ships had also been landed. The bombardment continued throughout the day. It transpired that the Arab forces were not much help. Wilson comments, kindly, that "although the attack was undisciplined by European standards, the Turkish garrison was eventually defeated".[19] The Naval Review's report is more direct:

18. *Lord Wester Wemyss*, 347.
19. *Lawrence of Arabia*, 352.

"The original intention was to use the Naval Brigade as a stiffening force, and to allow the Arabs to have the credit of actually taking the town. This did not work, however, as only about 200 followed Major Vickery and Captain Bray, two British officers leading them, and of those over 100 broke off and looted the first houses they got to: they found the houses packed with fair booty and made a sweep of it. They robbed the men, broke open doors, searched every room, smashed chests and cupboards, tore down all fittings, and slit open every mattress and pillow for hidden treasure: while the fire of the fleet punched large holes in every prominent wall or building. In short the town was in a woeful mess, almost uninhabitable, when its people returned from the hills."[20] "The remainder of the Arab force sat on the beach and refused to budge. The following morning at dawn the landing party advanced and occupied Wejh, but the bulk of the enemy force had got away during the night and only slight resistance was offered. Some eighty prisoners were taken with the town. The Arab army came up the next day, having been delayed by water difficulties, which a ship had to be sent down the coast to rectify."[21]

The capture of Wejh was a significant advance for the revolt in that it threatened the Hejaz Railway, thus paralysing the Turks and caused the Billi tribe to change allegiance, join Feisal and support the Revolt. However, it was not an ideal port for supplies from the sea, being very small:

"The harbour is about three cables long in the north easterly direction, rectangular in shape and has an entrance 250 yards wide between the reefs ... It is easy of access; no dangers bar the approach. A few stone houses marking the village of Wejh

20. *Lawrence of Arabia*, 162.
21. *Naval Operations in the Red Sea, 1916–17*, 659.

are on the northern shore. There is only room for one vessel of moderate size; such a vessel should moor head and stern close inside the northern point of the Bay where the bottom is of stiff clay."[22]

Despite the difficulties that this caused, Wejh became an important base: Egyptian troops were landed, aircraft, armoured cars and all the necessary stores were moved by ship over the following weeks.

It is again apparent that, without the actions and support of the Red Sea Patrol, it is unlikely that Wejh would have been taken when it was and that, most certainly, it could not have been sustained without all the equipment and stores that were brought in by sea. This was underlined by Lawrence:

"The capture of Wejh, which had been a foregone conclusion when once the Navy showed itself so willing to help, gave us what we wanted."[23]

22. *Red Sea and Gulf of Aden Pilot*, 301.
23. *Lawrence of Arabia*, 162.

Chapter Seven

Wejh to Akaba and Beyond:
January 1917–December 1918

HMS Lunka

In peacetime colours, as part of British India
Steam Navigation Company's Eastern fleet.

The day after Wejh fell to the Naval landing party, with Arab support, *Hardinge* went south to Sherm Habbam to take water to Feisal's army, before it could advance the last ten miles to Wejh. In addition to the late arrival of Feisal, another aspect of the Arabs' mode of fighting had been observed and commented on by the Naval Review and others (see last chapter):

"Afterwards there was looting. Lawrence noted in his diary: 'At Wejh the people of the town are all Egyptian ... and strongly anti-Sharif. So the Bisha men robbed them, and sacked the town: they broke every box and cupboard, tore down all fittings, cut open every mattress and cushion for gold ... Faisal had sent word to Wejh the week before, that if they stayed in the town and let the Turks stay, the resulting damage would be on their own heads. So he made no effort to recover their goods.' Despite the success, both Vickery and Bray were deeply shocked by the style of Arab warfare they had witnessed. Both were to write bitterly of the lack of discipline and planning. For example, Vickery noted that although Feisal's army 'only embarked on a four days march, due north, parallel to the coastline, and within 20 miles of it, a great part ... lost its way and arrived at the rendezvous two days late'."[1]

The next day, the 25th, *Hardinge* embarked twenty-five Turkish prisoners of war and the ratings of the naval landing party. She then spent two days discharging supplies before Colonel Wilson and Lawrence embarked for passage to Suez. Once they had been landed, together with the Turkish prisoners of war, and *Hardinge* had loaded yet more stores and taken on coal, she returned to Wejh, arriving there on the last day of January.

Boyle wrote to Wemyss on 5 February:

"... after your departure from Wej and the occupation of that town, the *Hardinge* remained to day nurse the Arabs and I went with *Fox* to settle the *Bacchus* question and then to Port Sudan to see about the W/T ... I was in Rabegh yesterday and Scott tells me that *El Kahira* should be able to do the necessary distilling on Monday (today) or tomorrow 6th. The pipeline is laid and a gangway built out so that when she is moored in *Bacchus*'

---

1. quoted in *Lawrence of Arabia*, 352.

present position the soldiers can walk to the shore ... Turton and I changed commands on Saturday and he left at once [with *Fox*] for Aden ... Arriving at Wej today, 200 Turkish prisoners will be turned over to the *Hardinge* for Suez ... and then 400 Arabs are to embark to attack Dhaba [Diba] from the sea. 700 are also moving by land but with the remembrance of our last experience it seems improbable the collaboration will be very effective. However, the 400 are going to attack if the land force have not arrived, at least so they say. I wonder. Mowillah I hope will then be gone for and as soon as that is through I propose going to Aden to settle the question of the launch *Kamaran* ... *M31* has been a long time at Yenbo and I have arranged for her to go back to Suez with the *Lama* on the 21st. She is of course very useful on the coast for the purpose of keeping up communication particularly now ships are scarcer, so that if you do not need her perhaps you would let me have her again, although I cannot think her guns will ever be required. With the occupation of these more northern ports clamour for ships is likely to increase and my intention is to station a vessel further north and cut out say Yenbo which can be visited occasionally."

He ends his letter with a plea for a transfer.

"It has been on my mind for some time to ask you to recommend me for a ship in home waters later on in the Spring ... In June I shall have been four years out of England which may excuse me for mentioning this but I confess my real reason is to take a more active part in the war before it finishes. As you know I have seen nothing yet and my being sent to the oldest and smallest Captain's command when I left Rome and one so far removed from the naval war was not exactly a compliment."[2]

---

2. Wemyss papers 4/4(1).

His plea was noted, although not until October 1917, when he was transferred to command HMS *Repulse,* a battle cruiser, under two years old. With a top speed of thirty-four knots (her sister ship, the *Renown* was reported to have reached forty-one knots in service) she was a far cry from the *Fox*. Although she was in the "naval war", described by Boyd, by then there was little more action than there was in the Red Sea.

The build-up of Wejh as a base continued throughout February. *Espiegle* was patrolling the coast when not at Wejh and was instrumental in the creation of a radio telegraphy station ashore. Boyle commented that this was "largely due to the indefatigable efforts of the captain of the sloop *Espiegle*, Commander R. Fitzmaurice, who was always to the fore when difficulties or dangers arose."[3] Boyle had a more favourable view of *Espiegle* and her captain than did Storrs (see Chapter 5).

At the beginning of February Boyle changed ships. He took command of *Northbrook*, and Turton went from *Northbrook* to *Fox* which sailed to Aden and was then active in the Southern Red Sea until the end of April. Once Wejh had been taken and reinforced, Feisal spent much time negotiating with local Arab leaders before advancing further; at the same time raids were organised on the Hejaz railway led by British officers. The importance of Wejh grew further; all the Egyptian troops supporting the Revolt moved there and a water distillation ship was based in the harbour to provide freshwater for all those ashore. Three days after Boyle had taken command of *Northbrook*, on 6 February they embarked 200 Arabs with rifles and ammunition and, in company with *Espiegle,* sailed to Diba, some sixty-five miles further north along the coast. They arrived the next morning and discharged the Arabs and a Naval landing party. *Espiegle* noted in her log that a white flag was seen as they arrived. After an hour and a quarter the landing party and the Arabs returned with thirty prisoners of war, having captured the town and defeated the Turkish garrison. The two ships then sailed on a

---

3. *My Naval Life*, 103.

further twenty-five miles north to Mowila (or Muheila) and anchored there in the early afternoon. Here the Turkish garrison evacuated the town and the Fort as they arrived. They stayed until the next morning. By securing Diba and Mowila all the coast of the of the eastern coast of the Red Sea from Qunfunda, south of Jeddah, up to the Straits of Tiran (the entrance to the Gulf of Aqaba and only forty miles from Mowila) was under the control of the Red Sea Patrol. During February a train was blown up for the first time by the Arab forces which increased the Turkish fears for the maintenance of their lines of communication. It was during one of these raids that the Arabs admitted to the British military officer with them that they were

"… out for British gold, not the Grand Sharif. Owing to the practice earlier in the movement, of paying the monthly subsidy in sovereigns, they had become the most common coins in circulation. On one occasion an Arab came down to a ship's boat and offered the bowman a sovereign for cigarette papers. The sailor, although surprised, rose to the occasion."[4]

Northbrook returned to anchor off Wejh, briefly, to put ashore the prisoners of war taken at Diba; she then went on to Rabegh, Jeddah and Port Sudan. *Northbrook* then sailed down to Aden and was on patrol in the southern part of the Red Sea for a period. The ships in the northern part had seen the action of the Red Sea campaign; those in the southern part had had a much less eventful time, with the only excitement coming from the dhows which were trying to evade the British blockade. Many dhows were captured by the launch *Kamaran*, which had belonged to the pilgrim station at Kameran Island but had been requisitioned by the Navy and put to work as part of the Red Sea Patrol. She was commanded by a Petty Officer Duke, with a crew of four British sailors, three Afghan fireman and a Maltese engineer

---

4. *Naval Operations in the Red Sea 1916–17*, 661.

(her former skipper/engineer), who also acted as an interpreter. Petty Officer Duke gained such a reputation along the southern part of the coast that he would go into port and order out the dhows suspected of smuggling, who would obey without argument. On one occasion he arrived at Kameran Island towing a string of ten captured dhows. He was so successful in his command of the *Kamaran* that he was promoted to Chief Petty Officer, Vice Admiral Wemyss having sent a signal to all ships of the Red Sea Patrol to inform them and also that he would be recommended for a decoration.

Northbrook found some excitement of her own in the Southern Red Sea. In the last week of February, after Boyle had rejoined *Fox* and Turton had regained command of *Northbrook*, she was involved in the salvaging of the paddle steamer *PS57*, which had run aground. This included removing all the movable fittings and embarking nineteen of her crew. The little, old, Royal Indian Marine sloop *Minto* had also arrived on the scene to help. She prepared her tow ropes, and a working party boarded *PS57* to help the remaining crew heave the ropes on board, which took all evening before they were made fast. The working party and the remaining crew of *PS57* did not return to *Northbrook* until 0330 the next morning, during which time *Minto* had been endeavouring to tow the stricken ship off. Just before six the tow ropes parted. *Northbrook* sent a 3½ inch steel wire rope over to *Minto* as a replacement. Steel wire rope is very heavy and the operation of moving a coil of it from one ship to another was a considerable feat of seamanship which would have involved *Northbrook*'s steam cutter and a large number of men to manhandle it. It was accomplished by mid-afternoon, when *Northbrook* sailed for Port Sudan. *Minto*'s log has not survived but in the *Northbrook*'s log it notes that on arrival in Port Sudan two days later she embarked the stores and gear of *PS57* embarked by *Minto*. It would appear that despite *Minto*'s best efforts – she was not only small but nearly 25 years old and a very similar ship to *Espiegle* in both appearance and horsepower – she had not been successful.

Also in February, the German raider *Wolf* was operating in the northern Indian Ocean. As a result two ships were employed to patrol in the area off Aden and the island of Socotra, to prevent any risk of the *Wolf* passing into the Red Sea. One of the weapons used by the *Wolf* was the floating mine, so a minesweeping force was formed, based in Aden. On 4 March *Odin*, a sister ship of *Espiegle*, was on a night patrol off Aden. She sighted a ship without lights heading for Aden, which refused to stop when signalled. The ship was chased towards Perim Island, where she scuttled herself at dawn. It was discovered that she was the *Turritella*, a tanker which had been captured by *Wolf* and fitted out as a mine layer. Her German crew of twenty-eight surrendered and the original Chinese crew, who had been made to help work the ship, were released.

Back in the northern part of Red Sea, in April intelligence was gained by the Admiralty office in Ismailia warning that a German officer had arrived at Aqaba and was in charge of laying a minefield offshore. Aqaba was by then, as Mohila and Diba were taken in February, the only remaining port north of Qunfunda still controlled by the Turks.

Lama, *Northbrook* and *Espiegle* sailed from Wejh in the early morning of 19 April together with the armed tug *Slieve Foy*. Boyle had decided that *Northbrook* had too deep a draft for the nature of the operation. So, just after 1600, *Lama* closed *Northbrook*, and Boyle, with a party of Egyptian soldiers and a naval landing party, transferred across to her from *Northbrook*. Together with *Espiegle* and *Slieve Foy*, the three ships transited the Straits of Tiran. After passing through they "darkened ship"[5] and made their way up the Gulf of Aqaba. Just before three the following morning they stopped and drifted in the still waters, waiting for sunrise. They stopped off Aqaba at 0550 and the landing party went ashore from *Lama* at 0600, covered by gunfire from *Lama* and *Espiegle*'s main guns. The Turks were driven out of their trenches overlooking the harbour with three killed and eleven

---

5. Extinguished all lights and covered all the ports.

taken prisoner. Those floating mines which had already been laid were found and destroyed by gunfire from *Slieve Foy* and *Espiegle*. Two boats that were found hidden ashore were destroyed. After three hours the landing party returned to *Lama* with the prisoners. The ships then sailed and were back at anchor at Wejh the next morning. The prisoners were taken ashore for interrogation by Lawrence as to the nature and manning of the Aqaba garrison; he discovered that the Turkish troops were of the gendarmerie rather than the regular army and were in fact nearly all Arabs.

On 15th May Admiral Wemyss sailed from Suez on *Northbrook*, with Boyle in command, accompanied by Sir Mark Sykes and François Georges-Picot. Wemyss described the latter as "one of the very nicest men I have met for very long time".[6] Other British officials found him less agreeable, describing him as having a "fluting voice"[7] and a condescending manner, and called him Picot rather than the name he had adopted.[8] Major Edward Cadogan, who was posted to the Arab Bureau in November 1918, had "a great deal of association with him. He was a tiresome individual, who, as so many of his race, was very anxious that the French should have as much kudos, and incidentally as much territory in the Middle East, as he could claim."[9] *Northbrook* took them to Jeddah where Wemyss was to meet Grand Sharif Hussein, who he described as "a nice old man, with a charming twinkle in his eye".[10] After his meeting and the subsequent meeting of Sykes and Georges-Picot with Hussein, they sailed for Aden. On passage, Wemyss' attention was drawn to the Turkish outpost of Salif, which sits on a rocky outcrop on the mainland, overlooking the Madiq Kameran, which is the strait which separates the mainland from Kameran Island. As the strait is only four miles wide, the town of

6. *Sir Wester Wemyss*, 353.
7. *Seven Pillars of Wisdom*, 510.
8. *A Line in the Sand*, 20.
9. *Under Fire in the Dardenelles* 142.
10. *Sir Wester Wemyss*, 353.

Kameran was within gunshot range of Salif. The decision was therefore made that it should be taken. Like the few remaining Turkish ports in the Southern Red Sea, it was supplied by blockade-running dhows, enough of which evaded the blockade to keep these few ports supplied. Another of those few small ports on the eastern side of the Red Sea, Dubab, which had resisted attempts to restrict its blockade-running activities, was attacked by *Northbrook, Clio* and *Odin*; a landing party destroyed the watchtower and approximately twenty dhows. They followed this success two days later by destroying another well-known base of blockade runners, Ibn Abbas, also on the east coast and opposite Kameran. Here another twelve dhows and a large store of petroleum and ammunition were burnt.

So, on June 11 *Northbrook, Topaze*,[11] *Espiegle, Odin* and *Minto* anchored off Salif. At dawn the next day they landed a party of 250 seamen and marines and successfully attacked and overwhelmed the Turkish positions, although with the loss of one killed and two wounded. A total of 127 Turks and Arabs surrendered and two guns and three machine guns were also taken. An account of this operation by Conrad Cato is more descriptive, although Cato's sources of information cannot be verified:

"The village of Salif is situated on a peninsula, … To the east of the village is a hunchback of a hill, which is doubtless a volcanic formation, and in fact has a hollow suggesting the relics of the crater. It was in this hollow that the Turkish garrison had taken up their position when, at daybreak on 12 June 1917, our ships approached Salif. The enemy's position was well chosen, for nothing could be seen of it from the sea and only the high angle fire of a howitzer could be expected to drop shells into it. Captain Boyle ordered the *Espiegle* to go northwards round the end of the

---

11. She was a small elderly light cruiser built in 1903 with relatively light armament; she was not a regular member of the Red Sea Patrol.

peninsular and enter the inlet between peninsular and mainland, possibly with the idea that the Turkish position might be more accessible from the eastern side of it. In any case the presence of a ship on that side would subject the enemy to crossfire, which is always disconcerting. The only danger to be avoided was that of the *Espiegle*'s gun layers, in an excess of enthusiasm, pumping shells right over the hill into the other ships; but unfortunately no contretemps of this kind occurred. The *Northbrook* anchored close inshore at the southern end of the peninsular, while *Minto*, *Topaze* and *Odin* made a line to the north of her. They all kept as near to the shore as the depth of water would allow, in order that the landing parties might have as short a distance as possible to cover in the boats. As it turned out the *Topaze* and *Odin* unconsciously followed the example of Lord Charles Beresford in the *Condor* at the bombardment of Alexandria, when he ran his ship in so close that the enemy ashore could not depress their guns sufficiently to hit him. The Turks in their hollow were in exactly the same predicament ... their shells, in clearing the sides of the crater, also cleared our ships and they did not score a single hit, though they occasionally dropped near enough to create an uncomfortable feeling on board. The *Northbrook*'s men landed at the south end of the peninsular, and took up a position near their ship to the right of the town. The others all landed at the pier, and extended themselves behind a ditch, flanked by a salt-mine at the south end and by some houses at the north end. They then advanced cautiously to the foot of the hill, making a crescent-shaped line around it, with a party of marines in the centre. The *Odin*'s seamen remained behind in the village (where there were no signs of any Turks) and took possession of the condensing plant, the telegraph office, some mines, and one or two harems belonging to the Turkish officials. The last named were transferred at the first opportunity to the *Northbrook*, which in due course took the women and children and the civilian males to Aden. Commander ARW Woods of the *Topaze* was in charge of the landing party, with Commander Salmond of the *Odin* as his second-in-command. His plan was to advance up the hill from three directions towards the Turkish position, and thus effectually surround it, for the fourth side was closed by the inlet from which the *Espiegle* was steadily pumping shells at the Turks. It is probable that the enemy, knowing that our force was a very small one, hoped to cause such havoc in it with their rifle fire while our men were coming up the hill, that we should be compelled to abandon the attack. If this was their calculation it failed to take into account the effectiveness of our gunnery.

"An excellent system of signals had been arranged, and by means of this Commander Woods was able to turn on or off a barrage of fire as if it were a water-tap. The gun layers were unfortunate in having the sun in their eyes, but, in spite of this, their shooting was so accurate that the men on shore could follow with confidence close behind the barrage. Under its cover they gradually crept towards the foot of the hill whereon the enemy were posted, and then, at a given signal, rushed forward and completely surrounded the Turks. The whole business lasted about three hours before the enemy surrendered. In justice to them it must be said that they put up quite a good fight ... Having captured the whole garrison, together with their guns, ammunition, and stores, and having placed the prisoners aboard *Topaze* for transport to Aden, the squadron moved off."[12]

Almost exactly a month before the action at Salih, Lawrence had left Wejh with Auda abu Tayi, the chief of the Howeitat tribe, with the intention of taking Aqaba. This journey was interrupted whilst Lawrence went on a reconnaissance mission to the north into Syria;

---

12. *The Navy Everywhere*, 291.

on the same day that the Red Sea Patrol attacked Salih he was at Ras el Baalbek, fifty miles north of Damascus.

The Arab force led by Auda abu Tayi and Lawrence eventually took Aqaba on 6 July. There was not much there. The Royal Navy had bombarded it on various occasions, starting with *Minerva* some eighteen months earlier. Jeremy Wilson notes:

> "They found little food in the town for their own needs, let alone those of their 650 Turkish prisoners. Apart from the ruins of a 16th-century stone fort, the place was merely a village of mud and rubble houses; its population before the war had been about a thousand. Supplies were required very urgently and as soon as the necessary defensive posts had been established, Lawrence set out with a small party along the old pilgrimage road across Sinai to Suez."[13]

Amongst all the planning for this raid, it appears that there was an assumption that food and stores would have been there for the taking. Unfortunately, this was not the case. Happily for Lawrence, who had travelled in haste to Egypt to beg for urgent supplies, and the Arab troops waiting at Aqaba, *Dufferin* had arrived at Suez on 10 July, with 100 Turkish prisoners of war and "eight undesirables", from Wejh. Following instructions from Admiral Wemyss, she loaded stores, two boxes of gold and a military escort of forty-seven rank-and-file in the morning of 12 July and sailed shortly thereafter for Aqaba, arriving there twenty-four hours later, landing the gold and stores. The next day she embarked 398 prisoners of war and returned with them to Suez. The disparity between the numbers of Turkish prisoners taken at Aqaba, which are variously recorded between 600 and 700, and the numbers of prisoners of war taken to Suez may be accounted for by the fact that some of the prisoners joined the Revolt. The *Hardinge* joined

---

13. *Lawrence of Arabia*, 417.

in the effort to supply Aqaba and 3,000 men with guns and animals were also transported to hold the place against any counter attack.

Whilst in Egypt, Lawrence had asked Wemyss for help:

"When we took Aqaba we were in a very dangerous state. I came to Ismailia and appealed to Wemyss in person. He instantly sent the *Dufferin* there with money and stores. She confirmed the weakness of the Arab forces, and the Admiral then sent his flagship, the *Euryalus*, to lie off the village as guard-ship for weeks. She was a four funnelled boat, and as such made an indelible impression on tribal opinion. Obviously, the more funnels the greater the ship. When the crisis had passed the *Euryalus* was, of course, withdrawn, but he replaced her by the *Humber* as permanent guardship."[14]

At this time, Edward Cadogan met Lawrence:

"I made the acquaintance of the famous Lawrence of Arabia. He was somewhat disappointing in appearance. He was very short – made all the shorter by the voluminous Arab robes which he habitually affected. I found him rather a *poseur,* but in many ways he was impressive enough. I got on very well with him."[15]

In reality, *Euryalus* only stayed at Aqaba from 28 July to 3 August, rather than the longer period suggested by Lawrence. On 3 August she was relieved by the armed tugs *Slieve Foy* and *Race Fisher*.

When *Euryalus* arrived at Suez the next day, she took the monitor *Humber* in tow back to the Gulf of Aqaba. Monitors were very slow ships and being towed by a cruiser (even *Euryalus*) would have cut the passage time in half. Once the two ships had passed through the Gulf

---

14. quoted in *Lord Wester Wemyss*, 359.
15. *Under Fire in the Dardanelles*, 142.

of Tiran at the entrance to the Gulf of Aqaba, the *Humber* was cast off to continue her passage, *Euryalus* transferring ten Egyptian army officers to her for passage to Aqaba.

This was the last time that Wemyss was to help Lawrence, as he had been transferred to another, far more important, post. Lawrence regretted his departure:

> "Admiral Wemyss was in glorious contrast to the soldiers – no jealousy, no stupidity, no laziness; he was as keen to help as any two-year-old. His support in the mixed councils and conferences was hearteningly useful. That was the main benefit he did us."[16]

The *Humber* was a happy choice to have been made guard-ship, as she had been built for the Brazilian Navy and was more comfortably equipped than ships built for the Royal Navy. Her captain, Captain Snagge, enjoyed his role at Aqaba, taking an interest in shoreside events and supporting Lawrence. The *Humber* was to stay at Aqaba until the end of 1917. On Christmas Day, Lawrence arrived at Aqaba in time for Christmas dinner aboard, as the British community in the port was being entertained by Captain Snagge:

> "... I took a ship from Suez in the little *Arethusa*, a four-hundred-ton coasting steamer affected to our service. We have three of these little vessels, and they were invaluable: though having been snugly built for the North Sea traffic they were hot as hell in the Red Sea for their unfortunate English officers."[17]

Little other reference is made to them and it would seem that they were chartered by the Royal Navy for transport purposes.

---

16. *Seven Pillars of Wisdom.*
17. *Seven Pillars of Wisdom*, 512.

Lawrence goes on to comment on a previous occasion when the Navy had offered warm hospitality:

"In the early days of the revolt it had been the *Hardinge* which had been given leisure to play providence to us. Once, at Yenbo, Feisal had ridden to the port from the hills on a streaming day of winter, cold, wet, miserable and tired. Linberry had sent a launch ashore, and invited him to the ship where he had found a warm cabin, a peaceful meal, and a bath made ready for him. Afterwards he lay far back in an armchair, smoking one of his constant cigarettes, and remarked dreamily to me that he now knew what the furnishing of heaven would be. My own private account with Snagge was of this healthy sort, many times repeated. Aqaba gave me many rides which were either too hot or too cold, many disappointments and pains: but he was always at hand with water, talk and food. Looking for stories to make him laugh showed me the funny side of my accidents ..."[18]

Various other works were, as usual, undertaken by the Navy to make Aqaba a useful and usable base:

"A good pier was constructed by the Navy, and a road [was constructed] by Egyptian labour who were sent for the purpose, the Arabs as usual, when manual labour had to be done, looking on. A large force of cavalry also came in overland from the South. At the end of July Feisal arrived and the whole of the Wejh base was shifted North (by sea) ... In the autumn the position was well established, and was made more secure in November by the arrival of Sharif Zeid with another 2000 men transported by sea from Wejh. From henceforth the Navy had little to do in the northern part of the Red Sea beyond carrying stores, etc. The

---

18. Ibid. 513.

campaign had lost its amphibious character, and developed into land warfare pure and simple."[19]

Although the activities of the Red Sea Patrol continued the Arabs were now in full possession of the northern part of the Red Sea and, as a result, the *Dufferin, Hardinge, Northbrook* and *Minto*, all ships of the Royal Indian Marine on service with the Royal Navy, together with *Lama* and *Lunka*, were gradually withdrawn to other parts of the world where their services were more urgently needed.

As a result there was now no ship which was large enough to carry the Holy Carpet with all its guards, cortege and camels from Egypt to Jeddah so, in 1918 the task fell to merchant ships, the *Pentakola* undertaking the task from Suez to Jeddah, and the *Mansourah* of Khedivial Mail Line taking them all back to Suez, both ships escorted by *Suva*. In the southern part of the Red Sea, the larger ships could not operate effectively because of the nature of the operation in the shallow waters. The operations were principally making sure that the blockade of dhows attempting to trade with Yemen and Asir, the provinces immediately to the north of the Aden Protectorate on the Red Sea Coast, was completely effective. *Espiegle, Odin* and *Clio* were useful, as they had both a shallow draft and armament sufficiently heavy to bombard towns several miles inland; *Espiegle* found that by anchoring in a particular place, which according to the chart was well inland, she could bombard the town of El Atn, which was five miles away inland. The importance of this town was that it had wells which provided a good source of fresh water for the nearby town of Loheiha, which was still in Turkish occupation. There were still three other Turkish garrisons on the coast, at Hodeida, Mocha and Sheik Said which were in the province of Yemen. They were considered harmless and remained in Turkish hands until the end of the war. There was a further action against Hodeida. On 25 June it had been reported that

---

19. *Naval Operations in the Red Sea, 1916–17,* 662.

there were two British and 200 Indian prisoners in the town in very poor conditions.

"Permission was obtained from the C. in C. to attempt their release, and the *Euryalus* on passage from Bombay to Suez was lent to assist. The *Northbrook, Euryalus, Topaze, Odin* and *Suva* anchored off the town before dawn on the morning of the 29th, and some 400 men were put ashore before daylight. It was hoped that when day broke and the presence of the ships and landing party were discovered, the local authorities would agree to liberate their prisoners under threat of bombardment. This, however, they refused to do and the government buildings were destroyed. The landing party advanced, but was subsequently withdrawn to the beach after having had 11 casualties, only two of which were wounded, nine suffering from heat stroke. In view of these latter and as it was then not 10 a.m., it was not considered advisable to advance again and the party was re-embarked. Although the principal object had failed the secondary was most successful. The population completely deserted the town and trade came to a standstill. The Turks who had a few 4 inch guns in position, fired on the ships but without scoring a hit."[20] (The subsequent fate of the prisoners is unknown).

Fox, now under the command of Captain H.A. Buchanan-Wollaston, who had relieved Boyle as SNO, had stayed with the Red Sea Patrol, but struck an uncharted rock and was towed off by *Venus* under the command of Captain Turton (who had previously been in command of *Northbrook*). Although little damage was done she took no further part in the activities of the Red Sea Patrol.

---

20. *Naval Operations in the Red Sea 1916–17*, 665.

During 1918 the seaplane carrier *City of Oxford* under the command of Commander John Brown RNR arrived in the Red Sea with her flight of planes, under the command of Flight-Commander Leigh.

"It was hoped that with her there would be sufficient incentive to the Idrissi [the ruler of Asir] and his followers to continue their activities against the Turks. But the effect of aerial operations was rather disappointing, as the Arabs seemed to prefer their job should be shifted to the shoulders of the Air Force. The direct result of the operations was a clearance of Turks from the hills and all the vicinity of Loheiha. They also made a successful bombing attack on the Fort at Zohrah, said to be the new Turkish Military HQ. The indirect result was a transfer of prestige from Turks to the Idrissi, to whom a number of wavering tribes sent important hostages in token of allegiance; according to some of these, warfare from the Heavens as well as on earth was not to be opposed. The Idrissi's increased confidence in and friendship with the British was very marked after the good work of the seaplanes. It must be added that our observations and photographs enabled a number of corrections to charts and maps of the neighbourhood to be made, not with precise accuracy, to be sure, but enough to facilitate navigation considerably."[21]

The last major activity of the Red Sea Patrol was in December 1918, after the armistice. The Turkish commander at Hodeidah,

"objected to receiving official news or terms of an armistice except from his own Government, and eventually a small military force was dispatched from Aden to offer final terms or forcibly occupy the place. The operation was an amphibious one; the approach and landing being managed by the Navy, who also furnished

---

21. *Naval Operations in the Red Sea*, 1917–19.

signal parties, store parties, all sea transport and necessary support by heavy gunfire. Six vessels led by *Suva* ... made up the Squadron, and among them was the *Juno* lent from the East India Station ... The ships anchored about daylight and negotiations commenced. The Turks were probably playing for time – anyhow negotiations occupied the whole day and broke down at dusk, when it was decided to land under cover of darkness on the sandy beach some distance to the northward of the town, and attack in the morning. A fresh south-westerly wind made the landing difficult and most of our soldiers were wet through on landing and had to spend the night so. The lee-shore was chosen because no resistance to landing was to be anticipated there, nor was any encountered. On the other hand the place was believed to be defended towards the southern approaches – and such proved to be the case. So the present difficulties and those obviously to come – getting boats and lighter off again – were accepted. The attack was successful and the place quickly occupied with hardly any casualties. One of the casualties was unfortunately an officer of the store ship *Suzetta*, killed by a 1 inch Nordenfelt bullet. There was some difficulty subsequently in landing mules and horses to the garrison, as neither lighters nor piers were suitable. The best way in the circumstances proved to be to heave them sideways unexpectedly into the water – of course as close to the shore as possible. One valuable horse swam out to sea in the dusk and was lost but it is believed that all remaining animals were landed safe and sound. Boats were used to turn them to the shore. The mules were far less trouble than the horses."[22]

After that there were minor mopping up operations involving the evacuation of the Turks, which were undertaken by *Espiegle*.

The Naval Review paper ends on a digressive note:

---

22. *Naval Operations in the Red Sea, 1917–19*, 55.

"Fish, birds, coral and shells among the reefs provide an endless source of interest and beauty. As to sport, the sea fishing is excellent in places; shooting is confined mostly to sand grouse. The Dorcas gazelle is plentiful in certain parts. There is naturally little time to attend these things in wartime, when the principal interest was dependent on the proximity of the enemy, the ramifications of political affairs and the Arabs themselves. Arabic life and language make the natives exceedingly clever at talking all around a point without reaching it, and they have scant regard for the value of time. It is said that the truth is not in them; it is there alright, however, but sometimes hard to get at. They have a very high standard of generosity and hospitality, and often even the humblest would not accept a tip from one they consider as a guest among them. But enough of these digressions. They will have served, it is hoped, to give an idea of the engrossing fascination of the Red Sea."[23]

Lawrence described the Arab Revolt as a sideshow of a sideshow; the Red Sea Patrol was perhaps operating in a backwater of that sideshow, but its effect on the Arab revolt was incalculable. As Lawrence said "The Red Sea patrol-ships were the fairy-godmothers of the Revolt ... I couldn't spend the time writing down a tenth of their services." Feisal's comment to Botha as to why the Arabs had succeeded where the Boers had failed was in the same vein:

"Ah, that was because you had not Admiral Wemyss and his ships to help you."[24]

23. *Naval Operations in the Red Sea, 1917–19*, 56.
24. *Lord Wester Wemyss*, 358.

Chapter Eight

"When the Time Comes to Tell of It"

HMS Clio

Sister ship to the Espiegle.

L awrence commented on "the value of command of the sea as a factor in shore operations against an enemy depending entirely on land communications for his maintenance".[1] The detailed inspection of the works of the Red Sea Patrol in the previous chapters has shown how vital command of the sea was in that campaign.

---

1. *TE Lawrence in War and Peace*, 217.

The ships from the Royal Indian Marine and the Merchant Navy, which are decried in some works as, in one case, "a slow steamer taken over by the Royal Navy"[2] were virtually all newer and faster than the warships of the Royal Navy that formed the basis of the Patrol. The "slow steamer" in question, the *Lama*, (with her sister ship *Lunka*, which was also part of the Patrol) a former British India coastal liner, had a top speed of nearly twice that of *Fox*, and was a significantly more comfortable vessel to sail on. The ships taken up from the Royal Indian Marine, *Northbrook*, *Hardinge* and *Dufferin*, were supremely suited to the work in which they became engaged. Built as troopships, they could, in addition to large numbers of troops, carry large quantities of stores. Lawrence's description of *Hardinge* taking on stores "8000 rifles, 3 million rounds of ammunition, thousands of shells, quantities of rice and flour, a shed full of uniforms, two tons of high explosives and all our petrol"[3] exemplifies their abilities. *Dufferin* and *Hardinge* had been fully employed from June for the taking of Jeddah, then loading stores in Suez and Port Sudan for Jeddah, and then returning to Suez with large numbers of prisoners of war. The gold necessary to keep the Revolt paid for also came down from Suez in the ships, under military guard. When necessary there was space on deck to carry horses, mules and camels, as when the Holy Carpet was transported in October 1916. Their last main effort was in moving Arab troops from Wejh to Aqaba in July and August 1917, when the two ships between them moved several thousand men.

The 4-inch main guns on those ships, the 4 and 6-inch guns on *Fox* and *Minerva*, the 6-inch guns of the monitors *M31* and *Humber* and the 4-inch guns of the smaller ships were of sufficient size to act as long-range artillery; the larger ships of necessity anchored in deeper water and, as at Jeddah, Rabegh, Yenbo, Qunfunda, Wejh, Salif and Aqaba used them to reduce opposition before the landing parties went

---

2. *Hero*, 9.
3. *Seven Pillars of Wisdom*, 135.

ashore. The threat of the ships' guns in deterring a Turkish attack on Yenbo in December 1916 was instrumental in its successful defence. In addition to the ships of the Red Sea Patrol, Boyle had brought in the monitor *M31*. *Dufferin*'s and *M31*'s searchlights were able to light up the surrounding country, to prevent any risk of a night attack.

The seaplanes of *Ben-my-Chree*, *Anne* and *Raven* were also of great use. It was the seaplanes of *Ben-my-Chree* that provided the final straw in the fall of Jeddah. The calm waters of the Red Sea provided far more amenable waters for their deployment than the cold, rough seas of the North Sea.

Radio communication with Cairo, from ship to shore and from ship to ship was also enabled by the Royal Navy; *Espiegle*'s captain, Captain Fitzmaurice, was instrumental, in addition to the normal ship to shore signal traffic, in setting up a shore radio station at Wejh.

At every port that was eventually surrendered by its Turkish garrison, naval landing parties, of sailors and marines, were at the forefront. Ostensibly in support of the Arab troops, in many cases they were the ones that did the fighting; at Wejh, for example, of the force of approximately 600 Arab troops that were landed with the naval landing party as support, only 200 followed Major Vickery and Captain Bray, who commanded the Arab troops, half of that number stopping to join in the looting of houses and businesses. Approximately 400 remained sitting on the beach. The naval landing party took the lead, attacked the Turkish positions and caused the surrender of the garrison. The main Arab force, led by Feisal and Lawrence arrived twenty-four hours later.

The resourcefulness of the Navy came into play, building jetties to enable stores to be landed and repairing shore equipment as for example at Rabegh, when in addition to building a pier, they surveyed the harbour; and in Yenbo, where a water distillation plant ashore, which provided fresh water for the town, was repaired. In Jeddah the Navy relaid the buoys and rebuilt the beacons on the approaches, to improve pilotage into the port for the many vessels that were using it. Much of this work was possible because of the use of the ships' steam cutters (see Appendix 1). The expertise of the Royal Navy in amphibious and littoral operations had been tested and had succeeded without the specialised craft that were developed a little over twenty years later. Ships' boats and commandeered dhows had done the job of the later generations of specialised landing craft.

By October 1916, when Lawrence travelled to Jeddah, with Storrs, on *Lama*, the ports on the coast from Qunfunda in the south to Yenbo in the north had been secured and held, despite the threat of Turkish attacks to retake Rabegh & Yenbo. The work of the Red Sea Patrol in taking and continuing to supply and support all these ports, whilst also being able to provide firepower to deter Turkish attack was the mainstay of the Arab Revolt. There can be little question that without that support the Arab Revolt would not have been in a position to move on, again with the support of the ships of the Patrol, and take Wejh. Further, without the ships and aircraft of the Red Sea Patrol, Jeddah would not have surrendered and the revolt would very likely have failed in June 1916. If that had been the case, there would have been no revolt for Lawrence to assess in October, which gives rise to the last sentence of the introduction – that Lawrence would have in all likelihood ended the war in Cairo as just another junior officer.

If that had been the case, Lawrence would undoubtedly have found fame in another field after the war. John Buchan in *Pilgrims Way* said of him

"If genius be, in Emerson's phrase, 'a stellar and undiminishable something,' whose origin is a mystery and whose essence cannot be defined then he was the only man of genius I have ever known."[4]

But it wasn't; and Lawrence paid due tribute to the Red Sea Patrol fulsomely, being very aware of how essential its support had been.

---

4. quoted in *Hero*, frontispiece.

Without the Royal Navy's support the legend of Lawrence of Arabia would have been lost to the world; *Seven Pillars of Wisdom* would not have been written; *The Mint* would not have appeared. Possibly Air Sea Rescue launches would not have developed as they did if SAC Shaw had not been in the Royal Air Force.[5]

If the Arab Revolt had failed how would the Middle East have evolved? Turkey would have surrendered to the Allied troops without Arab help. The Sykes-Picot agreement would have come into force, with little prospect of Emir Hussein having any comment of his taken into account, not that much notice was taken in any case. However, as his sons would not have achieved any prominence in the Arab revolt, the creation of Trans-Jordan may have been under another ruler than Abdullah. His pro-British sympathies may not have been shared by another ruler; the balance of power may have shifted. Arabia would undoubtedly be as it is today with Ibn Saud's Saudi Arabia controlling the Hejaz and Asir, in a kingdom stretching from the Red Sea to the Persian Gulf. Feisal would have been unlikely to have become King of Iraq without the intervention of Lawrence and Churchill, who were both also involved in Abdullah's advancement. If Feisal had not become the internationally known figure, who appeared at the Versailles Conference, it would seem likely that a different man would have been chosen to drink from that eventually poisoned chalice.

The Arab revolt did succeed and the Ottoman Empire did collapse. That collapse signalled a change in the style of government that the region had enjoyed for centuries. Before the collapse Arab chiefs and Emirs were granted an element of self-government by the distant rulers of Turkey, as a practical way of controlling a wide spread Empire. (It was to a degree this element of self-government that fomented the Arab revolt.) The governments that followed, at first controlled by Britain and France and then by independent Arab states, were less obliging not only in the manner of government and the application

---

5. *Lawrence of Arabia*, 879–89, *Another Life: Lawrence after Arabia*, 148–213.

of control but also in the matter of religion; the Ottoman Empire had tolerated a wide variety of religions and cultural ideas. Under the new regimes a more "one size fits all" system of government came into being, lumping Bedouin tribesmen and town dwellers together. Were the arbitrary lines drawn by Sykes and Picot, although earlier condemned, not much less arbitrary in their way than the independent states that later developed?

Finally, for the whole of the period that the Red Sea Patrol was supporting the Arab Revolt and sailing from Suez and Port Sudan to the eastern shore of the Red Sea, millions of tons of international shipping were sailing up and down the Red Sea to and from the Suez Canal, as trade continued throughout the war. To all that passing shipping the events on the eastern shore would have been of little concern. It was, to repeat Lawrence's words, "a sideshow of a sideshow" and the naval involvement was but a sideshow of that – but with a profound and far-reaching result.

The Steam Cutter

The steam cutter was the pre-eminent workhorse of the Royal Navy of the late nineteenth and early twentieth century. Part of the inventory of all but the smallest ships, it provided a platform which could be used for transporting men and stores from ship to shore and vice versa; mounted with a Maxim in the fore-part, it was a very capable small fighting craft. They were normally commanded by a midshipman, who would in all likelihood have been about 18 or 19 years old, with an experienced Petty Officer or Leading Seaman as second-in-command and a crew of approximately six, which would have included a Stoker in charge of the engine. It was a first command for many midshipmen and gave early responsibility for the command of a boat and its crew.

Cutters were built in many shipyards around Britain, to a range of standard designs. Of carvel or double diagonal timber construction (that is to say, with planks abutting each other, not overlapping as in clinker construction), the plans show a practical design, with an open cockpit aft, and the coal-fired boiler and engine located amidships, giving a top speed of 8 knots. The draft is not shown on the plan but would appear to be about two feet. A mounting for the heavy machine gun is shown on the foredeck. The remainder of the ships' boats would have been sail powered, so could be used where necessary to carry troops and stores and be towed by a steam cutter, of which larger ships would have had more than one. From the logs of the ships of the Red Sea Patrol it appeared that each of the ships present had only one steam cutter. The logs show that normal practice was for the steam to be raised on the cutter's boiler about 0400; the fires would then be damped down about

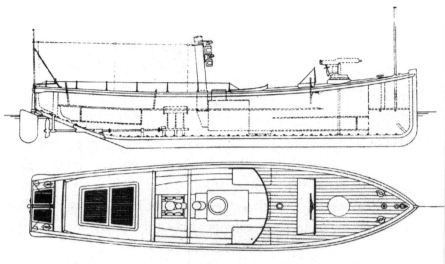

Section 5.   Type No. 28.   Design No. 2890.

Dimensions: 35 ft. × 7 ft. 8 in. × 4 ft. 3½ in.
Speed 8 knots per hour.

2300. The boat would then be ready for use throughout the day. At times of emergency, the fires would be maintained twenty-four hours a day, in case of need.

They were used throughout the campaign; as one example, on *Fox*'s visit to Aqaba on 3 January 1916, she had opened fire on the blockhouse at 0630; ninety minutes later the armed cutter's crew were sent to the blockhouse. Exactly a month later, back at Aqaba an armed party was landed by the steam cutter. In June, close to Jeddah, the cutter was sent to examine a dhow in a lagoon close inshore in shallow waters and returned to *Fox* having set fire to the dhow. The searching of dhows by the cutters is a recurring theme throughout the operations in the Red Sea; taking a large ship alongside the dhow would not have allowed the boarding party easy access. The cutter therefore was the forerunner of today's high–speed RIB (Rigid Inflatable Boat) which is now used to intercept small craft.

HMS *Hardinge* – Claim for Freight Payment[1]

N early two years after the armistice, Lieutenant Commander (his substantive rank – he had been an acting Commander during the war) Linberry, perhaps reflecting on his wartime service in command of the *Hardinge*, perhaps conscious that the Navy was diminishing in manpower, and that his services may shortly be dispensed with, wrote a letter to the Secretary of the Admiralty:

Sir,

I have the honour to request that in accordance with the Order-in-Council of 10th August 1888 their Lordships will be pleased to allow me Freight Money for the conveyance of gold and silver for the Arabian Government from the 23rd August 1916 to the 2nd November 1917, as marked A on the attached notes, and for the Egyptian Government on the occasion of carrying the Holy Carpet for Mecca on 24th September 1916 and 12th September 1917, as marked B on the attached notes, which were conveyed on board HMS Hardinge, of the Royal Indian Marine, under my command. I beg to submit that the subsequent Orders-in-Council dated 28th August 1914 and 24th October 1916 do not debar Freight Money being claimed from a friendly Foreign Government and that Rear Admiral Thomas Jackson, CB, MVO made the necessary engagement in this case, as required by paragraph 8 of the Order-in-Council of 10th of August 1888.

---

1. ADM1/8592/128.

Furthermore, I beg to submit that beside the additional responsibility assumed by me for the Arabian and Egyptian Governments I was also under liability to them, in accordance with the footnote to the Order-in-Council in the event of the loss of the gold and silver under my charge, to be liable for three fourths of its value.

I have the honour to be, Sir,

Your Obedient Servant,

T J Linberry.

The note marked A, which set out the dates of the conveyance of gold and silver for 1916 and 1917 gave a total of £199,000; note B, setting out gold and silver carried concurrently with the Holy Carpet for 1916 and 1917, gave a total of £51,900. The grand total carried in those two years by *Hardinge* was £250,900, which equates today to a little over £10,000,000. A successful claim for freight would have provided a very significant sum of money.

The wheels therefore started to turn in the Admiralty relatively quickly. On 30 September a note from the Naval Accountant-General's office stated:

"It is understood that no payment can be made in respect of the conveyance of this treasure but it is presumed that you prefer to report on this paper."

This was followed, on 16 October by:

"submitted to reply that the Order-in-Council of 10 August 1888 was annulled by an Order-in-Council of 26 October 1914 and the freight is no longer payable for the conveyance of treasure in Her Majesty's Ships."

On the 18th October, a different writer added:

"Correct. But was anything reported at the time as to the freight of this bullion? If, as I suppose was the case, the Royal Navy took the risk we could have claimed at least 25/- (£1.25) per hundredweight from the owners".

Hardinge had carried thirty-seven cases of bullion; the sums of money involved were starting to look significant. A further note on 9 December commented:

"Every effort has been made to trace an application from this office in 1916 but without success."

Five days later:

"May it be taken that no claim was made by the Admiralty for the conveyance of the bullion in these cases."

The Admiralty clearly rested over the Christmas period, because the next comment was not until 13 January 1921, from the Accountant-General's office:

"No claim has been made by this department for the freight of bullion in these cases."

No reply from the Admiralty had been forthcoming by the beginning of March so Linberry instructed his solicitors, Messrs Stillwell and Sons of 43, Pall Mall, London to pursue the matter. They wrote a letter dated 10th of March in which they ask that their client "may be favoured with a reply...". This brought forth a response dated 22nd March:

"Gentlemen,

In response to your letter of 10th instant, concerning the application made by Lieutenant Commander T J Linberry, Royal Navy for permission to claim freightage for the conveyance of bullion in 1916 and 1917 at the time when the Holy Carpet was conveyed between Suez and Jeddah, I am commanded by my Lords Commissioners of the Admiralty to state that no record can be found in the Admiralty of the transactions mentioned by Lieutenant Commander Linberry except that mention is made in a schedule of Live Stock and Stores conveyed with the Holy Carpet in 1917, of a sum of £19,000, with no reference to any undertakings with regard to the risk of loss, but that in any case the Order-in-Council of the 26 October 1914 terminated the system of payments to Officers of the Naval Service for the conveyance of Treasure in His Majesty's Ships."

(A report, dated 12th March 1921 setting out the terms of this letter, with explanatory notes, had noted that "if the ship had been sunk, the loss of the Holy Carpet would have been far more disastrous than the loss of the gold.")

There was no further communication with the Admiralty by Linberry. Whether his claim may have affected his future career is unknown. As the "Geddes Axe" was about to fall on the Royal Navy, his timing may be have been unfortunate.

Bibliography

Primary Sources

National Archive:
Ships' logs:
Ben-my-Chree: ADM53/35187 – ADM/53/35192
Clio: ADM53/38068
Dufferin: ADM/53/40295 – ADM/53/40314
Espiegle: ADM/53/41034 – ADM/53/41047
Euryalus: ADM/53/41220 –ADM/53/41221-162
Fox: ADM/53/42082 – ADM53/42096
Hardinge: ADM/53/43765 – 43787
Lama: ADM/53/45975 – ADM/53/45996
Minerva: ADM/53/49449 – ADM/53/49449-135 & ADM/53/49462 – ADM/53/49472
Northbrook: ADM/53/52862 – ADM/53/52881
Perth: ADM/53/55066 – ADM/53/55087
Suva: ADM/53/61867 – ADM/53/61892.

ADM1/8411/39
ADM/1/8592/128

Churchill College Archive Centre, University of Cambridge:
Lord Wester Wemyss papers

HMSO. *The Navy List 1916*, London, 1916

Secondary Sources:

Books:
Anderson, Scott. *Lawrence in Arabia* (London 2014)
Asher, Michael. *Lawrence: the Uncrowned King of Arabia* (London 1998)
Barr, James. *Setting the Desert on Fire: TE Lawrence and Britain's Secret War in Arabia* (London 2006)
Bonney, George. *The Battle of Jutland 1916* (Stroud 2002)
Brown, Malcolm and Cave, Julia. *A Touch of Genius* (London 1998)
Brown, Malcolm (ed.) *TE Lawrence in War and Peace* (London 2005)
Brown, Malcolm. *Lawrence of Arabia, the Life, the Legend* (London 2005)
Cato, Conrad. *The Navy Everywhere* (London 1919)
Cleveland, William L. *A History of the Modern Middle East* (Boulder USA 2004)
Charatan K and Cecil, Camilla (eds.). *Under fire in the Dardanelles: the Great War Diaries and Photographs of Major Edward Cadogan* (Barnsley 2006)
Corbett, Julian S. *Naval Operations (History of the Great War) Vol.2* (London 1921)
Cork and Orrery, Admiral of the Fleet the Earl of. *My Naval Life* (London 1942)
Crossland, Cyril. *Desert and Water Gardens of the Red Sea, Being an Account of the Natives and the Shore Formations of the Coast* (London 1913, reprinted Delhi 2009)
Dittmar FJ and Colledge JJ. *British Warships 1914-1919* (Shepperton 1972)
Garnett, David (ed.) *The Letters of TE Lawrence* (London 1938)
Graves, Robert. *Lawrence and the Arabs* (London 1927)
Gregory, David. *The Lion and the Eagle: Anglo-German Confrontation in the Imperial Era Volume 1* (Woodstock 2012)
Grove, Eric J. *The Royal Navy* (Basingstoke 2005)
Gunn, David. *Sailor in the Desert* (Barnsley 2013)
Gwatkin Williams, Captain RS, RN. *Under the Black Ensign* (London, undated)
Hattendorff, JB (ed.). *Oxford Encyclopaedia of Maritime History* (Oxford 2007)
Haws, Duncan. *Merchant Fleets: British India Steam Navigation Company* (Burwash 1987)
Hill, Rear Admiral R. *War at Sea in the Ironclad Age* (London 2002)
Humble, Richard. *Fraser of North Cape* (London 1983)
Hydrographic Office, Admiralty. *Red Sea and Gulf of Aden Pilot* (London 1909)
Kane, PJ and Hopkins, AG. *British Imperialism, Innovation and Expansion, 1688–1914* (London 1993)
James, Lawrence. *The Golden Warrior: the Life and Legend of Lawrence of Arabia* (London 1996)
Jamieson, Rear Admiral Sir William. *The Fleet that Jack Built* (Penzance 2004)
Jane, Fred T. (ed.) *Jane's Fighting Ships 1914* (1914, reprinted Newton Abbott 1968)

Jane's Fighting Ships of World War I (1919, reprinted New York 1990)

Knightley, Philip and Simpson, Colin. *The Secret Lives of Lawrence of Arabia* (London 1969)

Korda, Michael. *Hero: the Life and Legend of Lawrence of Arabia* (London 2012)

Lambert, Nicolas A. *Sir John Fisher's Naval Revolution* (Columbia USA 2002)

Lawrence, TE. *The Seven Pillars of Wisdom* (1922 text) (Fordingbridge 2003)

Lawrence, TE. *The Mint by 352087 A/C Ross* (London 1955)

Lyn, David. *The Ship: Steam, Steel and Torpedoes* (London 1980)

Mack, John E. *A Prince of our Disorder: the life of TE Lawrence* (London 1976)

Murphy, David. *The Arab Revolt 1916–18: Lawrence Sets Arabia Ablaze* (Oxford 2008)

Norman, Andrew. *TE Lawrence: Unravelling the Enigma* (Tiverton 2003)

Paine, Lincoln. *The Sea and Civilisation: A Maritime History of the World* (London 2014)

Schneer, Jonathan. *The Balfour Declaration: the origins of the Arab-Israeli Conflict* (London 2010)

Simpson, Andrew RB. *Another Life: Lawrence after Arabia* (Stroud 2008)

Sridheran, Rear Admiral K. *A Maritime History of India* (New Delhi 1982)

Storrs, Ronald. *Orientations* (London 1945)

Stuart, Desmond. *TE Lawrence: a New Biography* (New York 1977)

Thomas, Lowell. *With Lawrence in Arabia* (London, undated)

Temple Patterson, A. *Tyrwhitt of the Harwich Force* (London 1973)

White, Colin (ed.) *The Nelson Companion* (Stroud 1995)

Wilson, Ben. *Empire of the Deep: the Rise and Fall of the British Navy* (London 2013)

Wilson, Jeremy. *Lawrence of Arabia: the Authorised Biography of TE Lawrence* (London 1989)

Wemyss, Lady Wester. *The Life and Letters of Lord Wester Wemyss, Admiral of the Fleet* (London 1935)

Yardley, Michael. *TE Lawrence: a Biography* (New York 2000)

Unpublished Work

Lilley, Commander Terence D, RNR. "Operations of the 10th Cruiser Squadron: A Challenge for the Royal Navy & its Reserves" (PhD Thesis, University of Greenwich, 2012)

Articles:

Gilbert, Gregory P. "HMS Suva, Captain WHD Boyle and the Red Sea Patrol 1916–18: The Strategic Effects of an Auxiliary Cruiser upon the Arab Revolt" in the *International Journal of Naval History, Vol.8, No.1, 2009*

"Naval Operations in the Red Sea 1916-17" (anon.) in *The Naval Review, Vol.13, No. 4, 1925*

"Naval Operations in the Red Sea 1917-19" (anon.) in *The Naval Review Vol.14, No 1, 1926*

Weissman, Norbert. "Depictions of Indo-Arabic Charts on an Eighteenth Century Chart" in *Mariners Mirror, Vol 98:4*

Websites:

www.oca.269squadron.btinternet.co.uk/history/squadron_history/chronology/1914-1919.htm

www.adam-matthews-publications.co.uk/digital_guides/middle_east_politics_and_diplomacy:1904-1956

www.defencejournal.com/2001/july/forgotten.htm. "When the 62nd Punjabis along with Allied warships saved the Suez Canal"

Index

Abdul Aziz Ibn Saud, (xv)
Abdullah, Sharif, 30
Aboukir, HMS, 12
Abu Zenima, 53
Accountant-General, 130
Aden, 16, 29, 46, 91, 105
Admiral Hipper, 24
Agincourt, HMS, 34
Air Sea Rescue Launches, 125
Alexandretta, 27
Alexandria, 3
Ali, Sharif, 30, 64, 75, 85, 89–90
Allenby, Gen, (xiv)
Anne, HMS, 16–17, 19, 73, 85, 87,
  95–7, 123
Aqaba, and Gulf of, 1, 33, 35, 50–1,
  53, 57, 105, 112–13, 115, 122
Arethusa, SS, 114
Asher, Michael, 17
Asir, 47, 68, 118, 125
Auda abu Tayi, 111
Aurora, HIMS, 13
Aziz el Masri, 82

Bab-el-Mandeb, Straits of, 1, 5
Ballah Ferry, 37
Barber, Lt Cmdr R., RNR, 20
Ben-my Chree, HMS, 15–16, 19, 25,
  54, 65–6, 123
Beresford, Adm Lord Charles, 110
Betts, Cmdr E., RN, 21
Betts, Cmdr, RN, 57
Borolus, SS, 58

Botha, Gen, 27, 120
Boyle, Capt William, RN, 13, 19, 22,
  24, 27, 46, 49, 56, 60, 64, 77, 83, 86,
  91, 93, 95, 102, 108, 117
BP Tankers, 4
Bray, Capt, 98, 102, 123
Breslau, SMS, 34
Britannia, HMS, 22, 24
British India Steam Navigation
  Company Ltd., 18, 33
Brothers, the, 5
Brown, Cmdr J., RNR, 118
Brown, Malcolm, (xiii)
Buchan, John, 124
Buchanan-Wollaston, Capt H.A., RN,
  117

Cadogan, Maj E., 108, 113
Canton, SS, 47
Carew, George, 40–2
Cato, Conrad, 109
Christian, Austin, 42
City of Oxford, HMS, 118
City of Poona, SS, 43
Clio, HMS, 13, 36, 38, 109, 116–17
Condor, HMS, 110
Cork and Orrery, 12th Earl, 26
Cornwallis, Capt, 59–60, 71
Cressy, HMS, 12
Criddle, Sub Lt RNR, 91
Crossland, Cyril, 6–7
CUP, (xiv)
Cuxhaven, 16

d'Entrecasteaux, 37, 39–40
Daedalus Reef, 5
Dakalieh, SS, 72
Daphne, HMS, 25
Dar es Salaam, 19
Dhows, 6
Diba, 103, 105, 107
Domville, Adml Sir B., RN, 26
Dorcas Gazelle, 120
Dubab, 109
Dufferin, RIMS, 12, 14, 22, 44–5, 51,
    53, 57, 59–61, 65–8, 70–2, 74, 83–5,
    87, 89, 92–3, 112, 116, 122–3
Duke of York, HMS, 23
Duke, Petty Officer, RN, 105–106

El Atn, 116
El Fardan, 38
Emir of Harb, 66
Empress of Japan, SS, 47
Enver Pasha, (xiv)
Erin, HMS, 34
Espiegle, HMS, 13–14, 21–2, 25, 38,
    52, 57, 74, 77–9, 97, 104, 106–11,
    116, 118, 123
Euralyus, HMS, 1, 12, 27, 44, 55,
    77–8, 83–4, 89, 113–14, 117
Excellent, HMS, 23, 26

Fakri Pasha, 74, 90
Famagusta, 57
Feisal, Sharif, (xiv), 27, 30, 76, 89, 93,
    94, 101, 104, 115, 120, 123
Ferguson, Lt Cmdr, RNR, 91
Fisher, Adml Sir John, 10
Fitzmaurice, Cmdr R., RN, 79, 104,
    123
Fleet Reserve, 18
Foch, Marshal, 28
Fox, HMS, 8, 13, 19, 21, 25, 27, 34,
    44, 50, 52–9, 61–74, 76–7, 83–4, 93,
    95, 97, 102, 104, 117, 122

Foxhound, HMS, 36
Fraser, Lt B., RN, 22, 35

Geddes Axe, 132
Glory, HMS, 54
Goeben, SMS, 34
Great Rift Valley, 5
Gregory, David, 17, 34
Gurkhas, 2/7th, 43
Gwatkin-Williams, Capt R.S., RN,
    20

Haldane, Col, 43
Hannibal, HMS, 23
Hardinge, RIMS, 12, 14, 22, 37–45,
    51–50, 59, 61–8, 71–4, 76–9, 82, 84,
    88–90, 93–7, 101–103, 112, 115–16,
    122, 129–31
Hasani (or Hassani) Island, 44, 52,
    54–5, 70, 88, 95–6
Hejaz, 30
Himalaya, HMS, 39
Hodeidah, 47, 116, 118
Hogarth, Lt Cmdr, RNVR, 59–60
Hogue, HMS, 12
Huguet, Rear Adml (Fr.), 50
Humber, HMS, 17, 113–14, 122
Hussein, Emir, (xiii),(xv), 30, 51, 108,
    125

Ibn Abbas, 109
Ibn Saud, 125
Idrissi, 47, 69, 118
Ismailia, 37–8

Jeddah, (xv), 4, 6, 29–30, 45–6, 55–6,
    59, 61, 63–8, 70–1, 80, 82, 89, 105,
    122–3
Jervis Bay, HMS, 23
Jordan, Lt, RNR, 91–2
Juno, HMS, 118
Jupiter, HMS, 54

Kameran, 47, 58, 82, 108
Kameran, HMS, 58, 103, 105–106
Kantara, 37, 39
Katib Abu Azuk, 37
Kent, Lt J., RNR, 21
Khamsin, 5
Khartoum, 57
Khedivial Mail Line Co., 58
King Edward VII, 10

L'Estrange-Malone, Sqd Cmdr C.,
  RNAS, 20
Lake Timsah, 39
Lama, HMS, 4, 12, 14–15, 18–19, 47,
  51–50, 83–5, 103, 107, 116, 122
Laomedon, HMT, 72
Lawrence, TE, (xiii), (xiv), 4, 15,
  26–7, 58, 67, 81, 83, 87–9, 92–4,
  111, 113, 120–1, 123–4
Le Matin, 11
Leigh, Flight Cmdr, RNAS, 118
Lennox, HMS, 16
Linberry, Cmdr, RN, 92, 94, 115, 129,
  132
Loheia, 47, 58, 116, 118
Lunka, HMS, 12, 14, 18–19, 69–70,
  116, 122

M 31, HMS, 17, 76, 87, 103, 122–3
Madiq Kameran, 108
Mahmal, 76, 78, 122
Mansourah, SS, 58, 116
Massawa, SS, 47
McMahon, Sir Henry, (xv), 51
Mecca, 30, 45, 56, 75, 85
Medina, 30, 73–5, 85
Minerva, HMS, 12–13, 22–3, 35–6,
  38, 43, 52, 54–5, 74, 84, 89–92, 112,
  122
Mint, The, 125
Minto, RIMS, 12, 14, 25, 47, 51, 68,
  105, 109–10, 116

Mocha, 47, 116
Mohsin, Sherif, 78
Monarch, HMS, 24
Montcalm, 50
Moresby, Cmdr Robert, RN, 3
Mosquito HMS, 36
Mowila, 44, 103, 105, 107
Murray, Cmdr M., RN, 19
Murray, Gen Sir A., 83
Muscat, 57
Muttra, 73

Nairing, SS, 72
Naval Discipline Act, 21
Norddeich, 16
North Cape, Battle of, 23
North Star, HMS, 96
Northamptonshire Regiment, 70
Northbrook, RIMS, 12, 14, 22, 44, 47,
  51, 58, 104–10, 116–17, 122

Odin, HMS, 13, 107, 109–11, 116

P&O Steam Navigation Company, 3,
  33
Pax Britannica, 9
Peirce, Vice Adml Sir R.F., RN, 28,
  50
Pentakola, SS, 116
Perim, 47
Perth, HMS, 77
Picot, Francois Georges, 108, 126
Port Said, 17, 28, 37
Port Sudan, 6, 26, 31, 55, 57, 83–4,
  40, 105–106, 122, 126
Portheau, 89
Prince of Wales, HRH, 55
PS 57, SS, 106
Punjabis, 62nd Regiment, 39

Qunfunda (or Kunfunda), 47, 68, 80,
  84, 105, 107, 122, 124

Rabegh, 6, 73–5, 78, 80, 83–6, 88–9, 105, 122–4
Race Fisher, HMS, 113
Raikes, Capt C., RN, 22
Ras el Baalbek, 112
Ras Malek, 8, 73
Raven, HMS, 17, 89, 123
Red Sea, 1, 3
Repulse HMS, 25, 104
Requin, 37, 40
Resolution, HMS, 23
Ritchie, Cmdr H.P., VC, RN, 19, 21, 70
Riyadh, (xv)
Robertson, Lt Cmdr J., RNR, 19
Rowe, Lt Cmdr, RNR, 91–2
Royal Air Force, 125
Royal Indian Marine, 11, 122
Royal Naval Reserve, 18
Royal Navy, 11, 114, 122, 124
Ruhi, 59, 71
Rust, Albert, 42

Said, Sheik, 116
Salif, 47, 108–110, 122
Salmond, Cmdr, RN, 111
Sambuks, 6
Sansom, Wing Cmdr C., RNAS, 19, 65
Scharnhorst, 23
Scotia, HMS, 84
Scott, Cmdr C., RN, 19, 82
Selborne, Lord, 10
Seven Pillars of Wisdom, 125
Shahir, Emir, 59–60
Sharm-el-Sheikh, 6
Sherm Habbam, 96, 101
Sherm Ubber, 59
Sinai Peninsula, (xiv)
Slieve Foy, HMS, 107–108, 113
Snagge, Capt RN, 114–15
Somerin, 59
Stillwell and Sons, Solicitors, 131

Storrs, Ronald, 15, 51, 55, 59–60, 77–8, 81–2, 104, 124
Suez Canal (xiv), 3, 31, 34, 71, 83, 122, 126
Suez Canal Company, 37
Suez, Gulf of, 1, 71, 79
Suva, HMS, 15, 19, 54, 65, 68–71, 73, 83–4, 86, 88–90, 93, 95, 97, 116–18
Suzetta, HMT, 118
Swiftsure, HMS, 38–9
Sykes, Sir Mark, 108, 126
Sykes-Picot Agreement, 125

T124 Agreement, 20
Taif, 60
Tara, HMS, 20
Taylor, Sub Lt, RNR, 91
The Times, (xiii)
Tiran, Straits of, 51, 105, 107
Topaze, HMS, 109, 111, 117
Tor, 44, 53
Trafalgar, Battle of, 9
Tsuchima, Battle of, 10
Turritella, SS, 107
Turton, Capt RN, 55, 104, 116
Tussum, 39
Tyrwhitt, Rear Adml Sir Reginald, RN, 16

Uganda, SS, 16
Umm Lejh, 54–5, 57, 88, 93, 95

Venus, HMS, 116
Versailles Conference, 125
Vickery, Maj, 93, 98, 102, 123
Viking, HMS, 16

Warren, Cmdr, RN, 92
Warwickshire Regiment, 70
Wedgwood Benn, Lt, 20, 65
Wejh, 29, 55, 57, 76, 80, 92, 94–9, 101–102, 104, 115, 122–3

Wemyss, Vice Adml Sir Rosslyn, RN, 27–9, 55–6, 74, 76, 83, 85, 102, 106, 108, 112–13, 120
White, Colin, 23
White, Lt Cmdr R., RNR, 19
Wilson, Capt John, 3
Wilson, Jeremy, (xiii)
Wilson, Lt Col C.C., 66–7, 70, 73, 77–8, 83
Wingate, Sir R., 67, 85

Wolf, SMS, 107
Woods, Cmdr ARW, RN, 111

Yemen, 47
Yenbo, 54, 73, 76, 80, 86, 89–90, 93–4, 115, 122–4

Zeid, Emir, 59, 60, 75, 92, 115
Zohrah, 118